SLOW

simple living for a frantic world

BROOKE McALARY

sourcebooks

Published by Sourcebooks, Inc.

P.O. Box 4410, Naperville, Illinois 60567-4410

(630) 961-3900

Fax: (630) 961-2168

sourcebooks.com

Originally published as *Slow* in 2017 in Australia by Allen & Unwin.

Library of Congress Cataloging-in-Publication Data
Names: McAlary, Brooke, author.
Title: Slow : simple living for a frantic world / Brooke McAlary.
Description: Naperville : Sourcebooks, Inc., [2018]
Identifiers: LCCN 2017051904 | (hardcover : alk. paper)
Subjects: LCSH: Happiness. | Mindfulness (Psychology) | Quality of life.
Classification: LCC BF575.H27 M393 2018 | DDC 158.1—dc23 LC record available at https://lccn.loc.gov/2017051904

Printed and bound in China.

PIL 10 9 8 7 6 5 4 3 2 1

Dear Mr. and Mrs. Jones,

I am writing to inform you of my withdrawal from the race to keep up with you. It has come to my attention that prolonged attempts to compete with you have been detrimental to my health, my bank account, my self-confidence, and my ability to feel content. This is a price I am no longer willing to pay.

I'm tired. I'm frustrated. I'm resentful. I yearn for the simple things. Lying on the grass and watching the clouds. Taking a spontaneous drive to the beach. Evenings spent beside a backyard campfire. The undeniable joy of coaxing a seed to life in the dirt. Family movie nights. Long walks to nowhere in particular. Writing by hand, for fun. Weekends not completely overrun by sports and parties and activities and events and places to be and to be seen.

It is abundantly clear that I have far more to lose by continuing to compete with you, and I now find my previous role untenable.

Please accept this letter as my official notice, effective immediately.

Yours sincerely,

Brooke

CONTENTS

INTRODUCTION

S ix years ago, I was as close to having it all as you could imagine. Married to a wonderful man, mother to a lively and lovely one-year-old girl, pregnant with our second child, running a relatively successful handmade jewelry label, renovating our home, and just returned from an overseas vacation.

Life was abundant with all the good stuff we'd spent so much time chasing. And I was utterly despondent.

Yes, life was abundant. Abundant with *things*. A double garage so full, it had never seen a car. Closets crammed with clothes I hated (never a thing to wear!). Cupboards full of enough toys to entertain an entire preschool.

Life was also abundant with other *things*: debt, anxiety, and stress. Life was hectic and hurried. Overengineered and overcommitted, disconnected and dissatisfying.

Rather than question our priorities or try to work out why we were so unhappy, we got busier. We added items to our lists of things to buy, things to do, and goals to kick. We kept buying stuff we couldn't afford. We continued digging a deeper hole, all in the name of keeping up with the Joneses, never realizing we were slowly morphing into the Joneses.

After our second child was born, I was diagnosed with severe postpartum depression. At my best, I was an automaton—efficient, unfeeling, completely emotionally detached. At my worst, I was a nightmare—angry, bitter, sad, resentful, and entertaining suicidal thoughts.

I remember sitting in my psychiatrist's office, recounting the previous day and the anxiety that bloomed every time I stopped *doing*. She looked at me and asked, "Have you ever considered doing less? Maybe slowing down a bit?"

Doing less? Slowing down? Seriously? Doing less was for under-achievers. Slowing down was for weak, boring people. Mediocre! Average! Ordinary! I was none of those things, thank you very much, and frankly was offended she thought so little of me.

But that seed of an idea had taken root in my frazzled brain. It wasn't until days later, when I found myself despairing at everything I had to *do* and *be* and *own*, that I even considered it a possibility. Do less? Slow down? OK. Maybe. But how?

Naturally, I turned to Google and found my way to Leo Babauta's blog *Zen Habits*. There, I discovered a man who had completely transformed his life by choosing less. He was adamant that letting go of the excess stuff his family of eight had accumulated over the years led to massive changes in his health, happiness, work, home, parenting, relationships, finances, and self-esteem. He was an unapologetic advocate for a life of less stuff, and he wasn't alone. Further research revealed there were literally millions of people who shared similar values, who were saying no, doing less, and letting go. What's more, they were saying that this life of less stuff, less stress, fewer obligations, and fewer pressures was actually a life of more—more time, more energy, more freedom, more joy, more presence, more connection, and more health.

As I sat in my cluttered office late that night, illuminated by the blue light of my computer monitor, my family sleeping nearby and my coffee cold next to me, I realized I wanted to be one of these people. I wanted to find a life of more on the other side of less.

Over the next twelve months, my husband Ben and I decluttered stuff with a tenacity we'd previously reserved for acquiring it. We let go of more than twenty thousand items from our home that year (yes, I kept track) and many thousands more over the subsequent years. (I stopped counting because it was quickly becoming a new, albeit different, obsession with our stuff.)

We slowly started making other changes too and regained our weekends by learning to say no, do less, and embrace the lost art of downtime. We reined in the mindless spending by questioning our wants versus our needs and began reevaluating what it meant to live a successful life. We started sketching out a long-term plan for self-employment, which included shuttering my jewelry business and letting go of the relentless hustle I'd convinced myself was necessary. We rediscovered contentment by turning to gratitude and living in the present more often. And gradually, we realized we didn't want to be the Joneses. In fact, we didn't even like them very much. So we opted out. And while imperfect and still evolving, we've never been more at peace.

We now have way less stuff, less stress, less anxiety, and less dissatisfaction. We have more time, more space, more fun, and more creativity. We have better health, better relationships, better sleep, and better adventures. We're now both self-employed, and while that brings with it other complications, we're living with the benefits of more flexibility, more freedom, more time, and more satisfaction in our work.

Lest you think that's one massive humble-brag, please know this: Did slowing down and simplifying make our lives easier? Not really. And certainly not in the beginning. Simpler, yes, but not easier. What it did do was put the important things front and center. We can now, most days at least, rest easy in the knowledge that we're giving those important things the attention, love, time, and space they deserve. And we can also see that those important things really aren't things at all.

Every week, I receive emails asking how we achieved this values-centered life. Turns out many of you are facing the same challenges

INTRODUCTION

my husband and I were struggling with six years ago. And believe me, I get it.

As homes get bigger and self-storage facilities blossom in the suburbs, we find ourselves obsessed with the acquisition of ever more: stuff, status, activity, likes, followers, friends, and money.

Catalogues arrive daily. Online stores ring with purchases made day and night. Retail therapy is mistaken for actual therapy. Social media is used to sell us new clothes, new lifestyles, new business opportunities, new health trends. Advertisements bombard us with the next big thing, making us feel inadequate until we relent and buy, just to fit in.

To paraphrase American actor Will Rogers, we buy things we can't afford to impress people we don't like. And we do it every day.

We fill our calendars with meetings and parties, lessons and classes. We bemoan how busy we are while saying yes to another commitment.

We do these things because we believe, on some level, they will make us happy. We believe that if we just find the right combination of stuff and status, it will perfectly fill the discontented hole in our lives.

But we are more stressed than ever.

We are overwhelmed by a relentless amount of information every day. We have blooming consumer debt. We have homes so large, we can't keep them maintained. We have breakfast and dinner in the car. We have weekends booked out for months in advance. We have forgotten what it is to have less. Less stuff. Less stress. Less expectation. Less to do. Less to be. Less to prove. We are hyperconnected and utterly disconnected at the same time. We engage with strangers on social media, but we don't say hello to our neighbors.

Whenever I have the opportunity to talk face-to-face with people about creating a slower life of less, the response is almost always the same: their shoulders slump as they sigh and say, "Oh, that's what I need."

Usually, that's followed up with the question "But how?"

This book is an introduction to why a slower life is a more contented one, as well as a practical guide to how to achieve it.

Because I understand how hard it can be to crave simplicity or a slower pace when your reality is of overstuffed cupboards, booked-out weekends, and a crammed schedule. And I know how difficult it is to move from the theory into practice without hands-on guidance.

That's where slow living comes in.

What Is Slow Living?

Over the past two years on the *Slow Home Podcast*, I've interviewed more than one hundred people who all have different views on what it means to live a slower life. From moving to the country to urban living, tiny homes to ethical consumption, self-sustainability to slow food—there is no one way of describing the external indicators of slow living, because there is no one way to live a slower, simpler life.

This book is about how you can choose to slow down. Step off the ever-revolving carousel of want-buy-want-upgrade. Opt out of the comparison games. Stop cramming a month's worth of engagements into a weekend. Refuse to live your life according to trends. Tread lighter on the earth. Create a home and a life that is simpler and slower and, most importantly, works for you.

Author and slow-living advocate Erin Loechner told me that to her, slow living is a duality of caring more and caring less—that is, working out what's worth caring more about and letting go of the things that aren't. Since embracing a slower, more mindful life, she cares more about being available for her friends and far less about dust bunnies, for example. In other words, slow living doesn't necessarily look like a certain type of house or a particular combination of color-coordinated outfits, and it doesn't need to involve baking bread or growing vegetables either. If you spend any time perusing #slowliving, however, you'd be forgiven for believing this is a lifestyle based almost solely on wearing washed-out neutral tones while walking through the woods, of timber floors and white walls and fashionably worn stove tops surrounded by beautifully aged chopping boards, artful lattes, and crumpled bedsheets on rainy days.

But really, I think Erin gets to the heart of it. Slow living is a curious mix of being prepared and being prepared to let go. Caring more and caring less. Saying yes and saying no. Being present and walking away. Doing the important things and forgetting those that aren't. Grounded and free. Heavy and light. Organized and flexible. Complex and simple.

It's about living in accordance with the important things in life. And more specifically, living in accordance with the important things in *your* life.

It's about cultivating self-awareness, letting go of the excess stuff in

our homes, learning how to live mindfully, getting in touch with our personal values, and choosing which advice applies to our circumstances, happily releasing the ideas that don't fit our homes, families, jobs, or values.

It's about life. The living part, specifically. It's about paying attention to it and spending time in the noticing. The hand-holding and the tear stains and the sunrises and the uncertainties. The love and the anger and the joy and the envy.

So while this book opens by telling the Joneses where they can stick their version of a perfect life, it actually has very little to do with them and everything to do with you. Because your important stuff is almost certainly not the same as mine—or theirs.

This is not a quick-fix book. I won't guarantee results in days or weeks. I've been making changes to my family's life for more than six years, and we're not there yet.

Because there is no there. This isn't a race with a start and a finish line. This is slow, imperfect, intentional, and evolving.

So that's why you're here. That's why I'm here. And I'm glad of it.

How to Use This Book

Just as there is no one right way to live a happy, fulfilled, values-based life, there is no one right way of moving from where you are now to where you'd like to be. Please don't waste your energy comparing your path to that of a friend, a sister, or the author of slow-living books. Comparison is a losing game, and I'd much prefer to see you run your own race.

I began the process of slowing and simplifying my life by dealing first with the excess of stuff in our home. I was far too emotionally bruised to subject my soul to much searching six years ago, so I tackled the least taxing area of my life by letting go of things we didn't use, need, or even want.

It was slow, invigorating work that gradually shed weight from our home and my head. But only after months of decluttering could I even begin to examine other areas of my life that needed simplifying. That's when I started to consider my thoughts, my calendar, my opinions, my systems. Over time, I learned how to practice mindfulness and to create rhythms for our home life. I incorporated simple-living ideas into parenting and travel, changed the food we ate and how we prepared it, started yoga, and began cutting back on single-use plastics. It was a clear case of my psychological state gradually mimicking my physical environment, eventually leading my family to an entirely new way of living—and for us, it was the best path.

One of my dearest friends lives a very similar philosophy to me these days. She embraces slow living, growing much of her own food, advocating for adventure and unplugging and making her own, and being a present and wonderful mom. And she came at it from the exact opposite end of the process, learning to meditate after a serious car accident nearly cost her both her life and that of her unborn baby.

Not until years later did mindfulness begin to make itself known in other areas of her life, when she began clearing out the stuff left behind by her dad, who passed away when she was young. That stuff had been an important family link for a long time, and it took many years to even consider examining it. And yet she did. On her own timeline. When it worked for her.

Opposite experiences. Similar destinations. Different goals. Similar outcomes.

There is no one right way, and the only one that matters is the way that works for you. So take some time to read this book from beginning to end, giving yourself insight into the different elements of creating a slower, simpler life. And when you're finished, I ask only one thing of you: come back to chapter one and work through the questions posed there. After that, it's up to you. Where to begin, what to let go of, and how fast (or slowly) to move through the process.

SLOW

one

START WITH WHY

You'd be forgiven for believing that my progression from complicated and hectic to simplified and content unfolded in a neat, orderly fashion. That the catalyst for change was reading Leo Babauta's *Zen Habits*, and once I'd devoured his archives and decided I needed to simplify my home, it all happened in a rational way. No self-doubt and no backsliding. But the truth is, I value your time, and frankly, I value mine, so the retelling of my story is both heavily abridged and appears far more rational than what happened in reality.

I f I were to tell the story in its entirety, it would be long, drawn out, ugly, messy, and frustrating, and you'd likely be convinced the protagonist was an idiot. You would have to endure long descriptions of her wandering mindlessly, stumbling often, walking in circles, trying to find the vague outline of the path she glimpsed earlier. Two steps forward, eleven back. Suffer burnout, slowly recuperate, find her feet, overcommit, become overwhelmed, burnout again. Rinse. Repeat. I was the slow-living equivalent of the character in a horror movie who you really want to survive but who does herself no favors by repeatedly making the same mistakes. Not checking behind the door. Thinking the villain is dead when he's obviously faking. Believing she's safe once she finally reaches the car… Come on, girl. You know better than that, but here we go again.

I wasn't an idiot—not really—but my story certainly isn't the neat, linear version. It is a messy, frustrating story of someone who takes her time learning lessons and is willing to take imperfect action anyway.

With the benefit of hindsight, I can now see that in those first couple of years of trying to simplify my life, most of my early meandering stemmed from the fact that I didn't know why I was trying to make the changes. Sure, I could whine, "Ugh. Life is hard. I need to slow down," but as for my reasons, my specific Why, I had no idea what was driving the change.

Truth be told, it had been a very long time since I'd thought deeply about much at all. It had been so long since I'd actually thought about the life I was living and the choices I was making that I didn't know what I thought anymore. I didn't have an opinion on things. I didn't have a personal philosophy or even a set of values on which to frame and build my life. I was simply existing.

I didn't know what I thought, and I didn't know what I stood for. And without those two things, it proved really difficult to make changes in my life and make them stick. I needed to find my Why, but I didn't know how.

Had you asked me what I held most dear in my life, what my highest priorities were, I would have unequivocally told you it was my husband and kids. Of course it was them. They were everything to me, so they were firmly planted at the center of my life.

I certainly wouldn't have said Facebook—or comparing myself endlessly and brutally to others—was a priority. I wouldn't have told you it was the acquisition of more stuff or the deep desire to appear successful. Because those obviously weren't my highest priorities. Except they actually were. Those were the things on which I spent my time and my energy. That's where my efforts went, and no matter how unconsciously it was happening, the uncomfortable truth remains that this was the life I was living. I'd completely lost sight of my priorities.

Will Durant said, "We are what we repeatedly do," and I was repeatedly comparing and acquiring. Hating myself for coming up

short and failing to see the amazing things right in front of me. I was repeatedly and mindlessly wishing my days away and lamenting all that I didn't have.

There was an enormous disconnect between the things I valued most and my everyday actions. Even back then, in my haze of depression, anxiety, and numbness, I knew what the most important things to me were, but I didn't live as though I did.

Consider Your Legacy

One year, I spent Christmas and New Year in the Canadian Rockies with my family. We had saved for years to get there, and it was an experience we will never forget. Aside from beautiful memories of snowball fights and watching our kids learn to ski, that trip holds a very special place in my heart, because it was a delineation point, after which nothing was ever the same again.

Banff is a beautiful mountain town, set in the Rocky Mountains of southern Alberta. A little busy and a little touristy maybe, but beautiful. We were staying in the slower-paced town of nearby Canmore but had come to Banff to soak up the white Christmas festivities (like true Southern Hemispherians).

As we wandered through a bookshop, I picked up a squat little book called *642 Tiny Things to Write About*, hoping to use our holiday downtime to rekindle my old creative writing habit. When we got back to our apartment, I flicked through the book of writing prompts and opened to a random page.

"Write your eulogy in three sentences," it instructed me.

The book may have promised 642 *Tiny Things to Write About*, but what it was asking me to do was actually huge.

It was a call to define—clearly and succinctly—the most important elements of my life. And while it was only asking for three sentences, in those three sentences and the image that accompanied them would be the summation of an entire life. My life. This wasn't a writing prompt at all. This was a *living* prompt.

The book was asking me to fast-forward to a time where my life had come to an end and fill in the blanks. To imagine a life well-lived, but a life well-lived on my own terms. And it was terrifyingly exhilarating.

It prompted me to take a walk through the next four, five, six decades and see what might lie in store (or, more specifically, what I wanted to lie in store). What did I want to see happen in those interim decades? Who did I want at the center of my life? What did I want to spend my time doing? Where did I want to live? How did I want to treat people, my community, my planet?

And the bigger, unspoken question was: What kind of a life would I need to live in order for people to say the things I wanted them to say about me?

As I sat on the lounge, thinking about the life I wanted to spend the next few decades living, it called to mind not only the words I wanted to hear, but also the image of who would be delivering those words—and to whom.

Right then, in an apartment in Canmore, with my family nearby and my heart full of experiences I'd only ever dreamt of previously, I sat down and started to picture my life and what people would say about it once it was over. I imagined myself as a self-possessed older woman (think foxy and clever, like Helen Mirren) who'd spent her last days surrounded by family and close friends. I had the kind of face that has loved hard, laughed often, and found the good in people. My eyes had sparkled, and strangers had shared their stories with me.

I saw my two beautiful kids, now fully grown, delivering my eulogy to a large group of friends and family, and I imagined I was someone who'd had an impact on the world. Not a massive, audacious impact, but an impact nonetheless, because I'd been someone who didn't wait for others to start making a change. I imagined my children telling jokes about my emotional side and my love of a backyard campfire. I pictured them sharing stories about the travels we'd taken, the adventures I'd instigated, the fly-by-the-seat-of-my-pants way I'd lived. The fact that I'd always had a good book, a big idea, and an embarrassingly ready laugh. I'd had a weird sense of humor, a genuine love of postapocalyptic fiction (the more zombies the better, truth be told),

9

and an inclusiveness. I'd been introverted and loved being alone, but I was always warm and open to the people I met and happy to put myself in front of them if I'd thought I could help. I had been a mother and a wife and a friend people were glad to have known and sad to see go. And I'd had the mature sass and silver hair of Helen Mirren. Of course.

After a few rewrites, I could get my eulogy down to four sentences. (I'm an overwriter. What can I say?) Here's what I imagined my children saying, God willing, at least five decades from now:

> Quick to laugh, creative, compassionate, with a wicked sense of humor, Mom was never without a new plan or adventure on the horizon. She made one hell of an old-fashioned, was spontaneous, loyal, introspective, and believed wholeheartedly that we all have a responsibility to leave the world a better place than we found it. Mom, we'll miss you always. Thank you for our roots, but thank you even more for our wings.

Imperfect and human, a poor imagining perhaps, but this is what I heard. This was the summation of a life well lived.

Now let me tell you what wasn't in that eulogy, what never even crossed my mind as I wrote those words:

- bank balance
- wardrobe size and/or fashionability
- the size of my pores
- regularity of eyebrow waxing
- floor shininess
- shoes and handbags
- kids' extracurricular activities
- acceptance into cool group
- flatness of postchildren belly
- smile lines versus crow's-feet
- beautifully curated Instagram feed
- number of Facebook friends
- smallest jeans size ever achieved

And yet I had spent a stunning number of hours worrying about these things, trying to remedy, forget, attain, or disguise them. I never thought they were the most important things in my life, but I often lived like they were.

Family, friends, purpose. Emotional honesty, fun, travel, adventure, spontaneity. Stories, creativity, laughter, warmth, generosity. This is what a life well lived looked like for me.

The question I had to ask myself was "Am I living a life right now that would look like that if we were to fast-forward about fifty years?"

The sobering answer was no.

Too much of my time and energy was spent bogged down in

comparisons, frustrations, and stresses of no importance. Not enough of my time and energy was spent in play, presence, bravery, compassion, adventure, acceptance, creativity, or love. I didn't even drink old-fashioneds.

It was clear to me that the important people, pursuits, and qualities were already present in my life, but they simply weren't getting the attention they deserved.

So then and there, I decided to start living life with those important things at the center. Making room every day for who and what matters most. Because, as that wise fellow Will Durant has already told us, we are what we repeatedly do.

Of course, not everyone has the good fortune of living to the age of ninety or looking like Helen Mirren while doing so. (In fact, I'd hazard a guess that not many of us will ever tick that second box.) I have no idea how my life will unfold—what fortunes or challenges await me. But this isn't a manifestation exercise where we imagine the life we want and then live in a bubble of entitlement, expecting it to be exactly like we pictured, simply because we wished it so.

By placing these priorities at the forefront of my mind, I have slowly created a life aligned with values that are important to me and my family, a life aligned with my Why. What I've discovered is that the Why needed to come first, while the How followed behind.

My Why took the form of a short eulogy, just seventy-four words,

Slow Old-Fashioned

1 Demerara sugar cube

1½ ounces rye whiskey

2 healthy dashes bitters

1 cup ice cubes

1 slice orange peel

1 slice orange

In a chilled old-fashioned glass, muddle the sugar cube, bitters, and a little water (if necessary) until well combined. Twist the orange peel over the glass to extract the oils, add the whiskey, fill the glass halfway with ice (the bigger the cubes, the better), and stir. Add the peel to the glass along with the rest of the ice and stir until the liquid is chilled, about a dozen times. Garnish with a slice of orange and enjoy slowly.

but those seventy-four words have changed everything. They've become a touchstone that I refer back to constantly. The words are my compass, helping me navigate difficult decisions and awkward conversations, and have given me the confidence to explain why I've made a particular choice. Having and knowing my Why helps me decide what actions to take, which issues are worthy of my time and concern, and which are not. Understanding my Why has helped—and will continue to help—steer me and my family through the inevitable challenges and obstacles that life provides and create a life much more closely aligned with our Why than if we'd simply left it up to chance.

I personally teeter on the edge of idealism, and it would be easy for me to topple into the question of why can't we all share similar values? And while it might be true that this would make things simpler, it would also make the world a boring, homogenous place. Instead, we need to work out our own priorities and go from there.

Focus on What's Important—to You

We're told—by magazines, social media, newspapers, catalogs, social commentators, influencers, trend forecasters, reality TV hosts, and the socially conditioned—that if we lack in bank balance, pore size, belly flatness, or cool factors, there's something wrong with us. We should be ashamed of our eyebrows, our floors, our aging faces. What I can tell you is that the moment I stopped worrying so much about what these external influencers thought is the moment I discovered contentment and realized just how much bullshit we're being peddled on a daily basis. So much of what we worry about simply doesn't matter very much, and yet we give it our time and energy. Imagine if we used that time and energy to focus on things that were important to us instead.

I'm not going to pretend I never give these things a second thought, because that would be an outright lie, and there are enough people painting incomplete and inaccurate pictures of their lives already (sometimes referred to as social media). But what I've been able to do since sitting in that Canadian apartment, writing my eulogy, and getting hit between the eyes with the biggest realization of my life, is to put those things at the level of importance to which they belong.

For example, shiny floors, handbags, and shoe choices now sit at a level 1 or 2: I *could* care less, but not much.

It's nice and tidy to be able to put things in a snappy list of what is no longer remotely important to me, all the way up to my level 10s. It also does no justice to the years it took me to find the clarity and confidence to do so. There have been false starts and restarts, failures and successes, and many tears of frustration to even begin to establish my Why.

Which begs the question: What if you've done the head work, sat down to write the eulogy, and come up empty? What if you feel like one of my workshop attendees, who approached me tearfully at

The Barometer of Caring

10 — EULOGY WORTHY

- Love. Family and friends
- People
- The planet
- Stephen King books
- Travel
- Sustainable living
- Laughter
- Gardening
- Good stories
- Kitchen dancing
- Snowflakes
- Comedy autobiographies
- French brie

-5- I COULD CARE MORE
(I just don't want to)

- Clothes
- Outward appearances
- Eyebrow shape
- Football
- Shiny floors
- Opinion dressed as news
- Current dietary trends
- Throw cushions
- Soccer
- Color of the year

1 — I COULD CARE LESS (just)

- Nail art
- Reality TV
- Clickbait
- Golf

morning tea to admit he couldn't identify any big Why beyond his work? What if you don't know what your Why looks like, or if you even have one?

In the midst of my depression, as much as I knew I loved my family and friends, I was so terrifyingly numb that I couldn't connect with them. I didn't have the ability to feel, and my inner monologue was doing its best to convince me that my family and friends didn't want me anyway. I knew there was more to life, but I didn't have anything beyond a blurry, foggy vision of what that was until I began to pay attention. When I looked closely at the times I felt good, the moments I was happy, the days I woke with energy or passion, I began to work out what inspired me and helped me feel good. I started paying attention to what I was listening to, what I was reading, what I was eating, what I was spending my time thinking about and valuing. And by noticing the moments I *was* feeling good, I was slowly able to realize why I felt good. Perhaps I'd spent uninterrupted time playing with my kids. I'd managed more than the average four hours of sleep the night before. I'd eaten a good breakfast and drunk enough water. I'd spent time reading or working on a project I loved. I had listened to a funny podcast and found myself thinking about things in a different way or with a levity I hadn't previously enjoyed.

In short, I began paying attention to the inputs in my life and started to understand that I was capable of improving the quality of those

In order to change, we first need to notice. To pay attention, not only to what is happening around us and the good things in our lives that we ought to be grateful for, but also to ourselves. To notice what gives us passion and energy, what lights us up and makes us feel good.

inputs—enjoying more of the things that made me feel better and less of the things that didn't. That's not to say it was easy (it wasn't), and it's only with the benefit of hindsight that I can even see that this is what I'd been doing.

Paying attention is the key.

Do the Work

Have you heard the term "to earn your chops"? It essentially means to do the work. To put in the hours and commit to the process of gaining skill or knowledge in a particular area. For example, to earn your chops in comedy means to go through the learning of the craft, open mic nights, bad gigs, awkwardness, imposter syndrome, copying, and finding your feet and your voice and your point of view in order to emerge on the other side with skill, insight, a sense of what works, and something to say.

(I know all this because I read both Amy Poehler and Tina Fey's books, as well as Judd Apatow's most excellent *Sick in the Head*. Plus, my brother-in-law has done stand-up for years, so I am basically an expert. In fact, I think I'm ready for my hour-long special.)

Learning to live a slower, simpler life was a similar process. I had to earn my chops. I had to figure out what inspired me, what I stood for, what I loved, what I was passionate about, and why. And while I didn't realize I was doing it at the time, the many, many, many hours of consuming information were the beginning of this process.

I uncovered hours of inspiration, motivation, and even aspiration on the digital and physical pages of Tsh Oxenreider's books and website. I unearthed the first fragments of my embryonic personal philosophy in the words of Courtney Carver, Rhonda Hetzel, Henry David Thoreau, and Carl Honoré. I also recognized slivers of personal truth in less obvious places, such as Amy, Tina, and Judd's books with their ideas on creativity and identity. The joyful, honest writings of Anne Lamott and the significantly sharper words of Stephen King both, to this day, form part of my personal philosophy, and I refer to them often.

Other unexpected places I've unearthed fragments of my personal philosophy over the years:

- *To Kill a Mockingbird* by Harper Lee
- *The Lorax* by Dr. Seuss
- road trips
- the slightly nutty ramblings on the label of Dr. Bronner's Pure-Castile soaps
- *Big Magic* by Elizabeth Gilbert
- *The Icarus Deception* by Seth Godin
- dancing

- Chris Hardwick on the *Nerdist* podcast (Stephen Tobolowsky's interview is incredible)
- Marc Maron interviewing Jason Segel
- "Fossils and Tin" by Shred Kelly
- *The Little Prince* by Antoine de Saint-Exupéry
- *The Wool Trilogy* by Hugh Howey
- Bronnie Ware's "Regrets of the Dying" blog post
- Stephen King's *On Writing*, *The Stand*, and *The Dark Tower* series
- *A Squash and a Squeeze* by Julia Donaldson
- Robin Williams in pretty much everything he ever did (especially *Hook* and *Dead Poets Society*)

What reading a book or listening to a podcast didn't do for me, however, was the work. It was very easy to convince myself that hours spent reading *Zen Habits* or immersed in whatever self-help book I'd bought as The Only Solution to My Problems I Will Ever Need was productive time. Don't get me wrong—inspiration is a wonderful tool to light a fire under us. But if all we do is sit there and let it burn our pants, then it's not all that helpful, is it? You've yet to make any changes, and now you need new pants.

People have been digging deep into what it means to live a contented life for many centuries. Ancient philosophers Socrates and Plato

ruminated on the "unexamined life," while Rumi gave us deep insights into the human condition that are somehow as relevant now as when they were written more than seven hundred years ago. Since then, there have been countless others, myself included, who have riffed on these same ideas and tried to apply them to modern life.

So access to these ideas wasn't the issue for me. I had access to all the information on living a good life I could handle. More than I could handle, actually. If anything, the amount of information was overwhelming and confusing, because it was contradictory or simply didn't resonate with me at the time.

The perfect solution wasn't lurking in the pages of a book, just waiting for me to unearth it, dust it off, and see how it fit snugly into the ragged holes of my life. No one was going to deliver a magic solution and help me live better.

I had to earn my chops.

I had to start somewhere. Anywhere, really. And while I wish I could tell you I started by diving into the process of discovering my Why, it's not entirely true. Uncovering my Why was the single most important step I took in clarifying my values and the kind of life I wanted to live, but it didn't happen immediately.

I'd read simple living books and spent countless hours perusing blogs about minimalism and decluttering. I was starting to formulate a notion of my personal philosophy, based on the quotes I kept returning to and the ideas that continued to rattle around in my head long after I'd moved on to another book. But it was almost useless until I actually started doing something with it.

Occasionally, at a workshop or a conference, someone will look at me with a conspiratorial smile, waiting until the rest of the people I'm chatting with have moved on. They'll walk up and introduce themselves, share their story and their reasons for wanting to slow down, and then they will ask me what the secret is. What do they need to do in order to make the process of slowing down as rapid as possible? What advice do I have for them in particular? And not the advice I give everyone else— the real, powerful advice. The secret.

And here it is: do the work.

Imagining a Life Well Lived

To be fair, it's actually pretty rare that I'm asked about the nonexistent secret shortcut. The far more common question is "How do I start?" and it comes from people who are simply overwhelmed at the thought of beginning. They're tired, stressed, overcommitted, and struggling to find any peace or simplicity in their day-to-day existence. They want to learn how, but they just can't find an easy entry point. It all looks too big or time-consuming.

Do the work of uncovering your Why.
Do the work of establishing your own
personal philosophy and set of values.
Do the work of naming the highest,
eulogy-worthy priorities in your life.
Then do the work of putting them at
the center of your life, every day.

This isn't really a workbook kind of book, but if I could encourage you to complete one exercise or task in these pages, it would be to consider your legacy. I know a lot of people find the idea of eulogy writing to be quite confronting, so instead, I offer the friendlier idea of legacy. I'd encourage you to take some time and consider what kind of life you want to be remembered for.

This is a deceptively simple exercise that asks some of the biggest questions we can face. So find a quiet space, a blank sheet of paper, and a little time, and ask yourself:

- What is important to me?
- What do I want to leave behind?
- What don't I want to leave behind?
- What do I want people to say about me?
- What regrets do I want to avoid?

Simply jot down your thoughts without censoring them. This is not the time to judge yourself or your answers; it's the time to listen.

You can start to circle common ideas, people, places, goals, images, and feelings, and if you want to, you can begin to put them into a few sentences that describe who you want to be during the course of your life. However you structure the process, simply be honest.

You don't need to show what you write to anyone else, and you are not signing a contract. You're allowed to change your focus; you're allowed to grow and evolve.

Write out a list of things that are at the center of your priorities, and then set the list aside for a while. Pop it in your wallet or your handbag. Take a photo of it, and keep it on your phone. As you begin the process of slowing down and simplifying your life, you will need to refer to this list.

This list will become your compass, and you will use it countless times to help navigate the decisions and conversations required to slowly bring your Why to the center of your life.

o o o

There is no quick-fix magic cure to a hectic, overcomplicated life; the closest thing you will find is to do the work of uncovering your Why and excavating your personal values.

The slow excavation of your own personal philosophy, your own set of reasons, your own yardstick of a life well lived will hold you in better stead than any magic cure ever could, because it is in the doing that we learn. And it's in the learning that we find our reasons. And it's in those reasons that we find our strength and conviction. And from there, you can do anything.

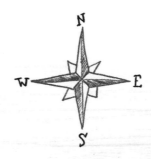

My Why

Take a moment to think about those things that matter
most to you—the things that light you up, make you smile,
or matter more than anything else. Write them down.

_____

_____

_____

_____

_____

_____

_____

two

DECLUTTER

In those first months after my postpartum depression diagnosis, I was in a pretty delicate emotional state. Raw. I'd stripped the lining of myself, and every criticism, every doubt, every stumble and moment of anger, every irrational reaction, every bad day felt like salt in a wound. Apart from the work I was doing with both my psychiatrist and psychologist, I wasn't in a position to make sweeping mental or emotional changes. I couldn't even bear to examine my state of mind too closely; I was too much of a mess.

Leo Babauta was my entry point into the world of simplicity and all it entailed. He wrote so beautifully and honestly about the efforts to change his mind-set and habits. And while some of the advice he was offering was way too cerebral for my mental state at the time, asking for more self-examination than I was capable of, he also wrote a lot about minimalism—the intentional removal of our excess.

The more I read, on Leo's blog and others, the more obvious it became that simplicity in our physical environment is a huge part of creating a simpler life. It sounds so obvious now, but when we're conditioned, as I was, to believe that we need more, bigger, newer, shinier, and that this is where success lies, it sounds positively exotic to think a life of less could be a life of freedom and contentment.

Making a Start

Ben and I were by no means hoarders and had what I'd say was a "normal" amount of stuff, but as we began to look at our belongings with a different perspective, I could feel all of them weighing on me. And they were heavy.

So I started decluttering.

The double garage in our backyard was internally divided in two—one half had been my jewelry-making studio and storage area (now basically abandoned and full of stuff that had nothing but negative emotions attached to it), and the other half was full of boxes. Boxes and boxes of stuff we'd packed up three years earlier when we moved to our new place. Boxes and boxes of stuff that seemed important enough to move with us but wasn't actually important or useful enough to have made it into our house. We would have been hard-pressed to name a single thing in any of those boxes, yet there they were, taking up space in our lives.

I assumed this would be a good place to start our decluttering journey. After all, if we didn't know what was in those boxes, surely it would be easy to let it all go.

One Saturday morning, Ben and I headed out to the garage, determined to get rid of this excess stuff. We each opened a box and started sifting through the contents, making a pile of things to keep, a pile of things to sell at our upcoming garage sale, and a pile of things to give or throw away. We'd pick up an item, put it in a pile, and move on to the next. It was simple enough until we arrived at an item we just weren't sure about, which we'd then put on a sprawling pile loosely known as the "I forgot we had this thing, but now that I've seen it, I think maybe we should keep it, but then again, do we really need it?" pile. It's hardly surprising that the majority of things in the boxes wound up in this pile.

As we continued to work through the boxes, sorting our stuff into ever-expanding piles but not actually committing to do anything with

"Be a curator of your life. Slowly cut things out until you're left only with what you love, with what's necessary, with what makes you happy."

—Leo Babauta

most of it, we realized we were completely overwhelmed. The piles began to merge. We'd open up some space by recycling a whole heap of papers, only to fill it with more "just in case" items that we didn't really need but didn't think we could let go of. You know, just in case.

After a few hours of shuffling and sorting and faux decision making, we were at a complete loss. There were piles all around, and we couldn't remember which was which. It was at that moment we called it quits, walked out of the garage, rolled the doors down, and felt completely defeated.

Perhaps you've heard the saying, "the definition of insanity is doing the same thing and expecting different results." Well, I'd like to tell you I was smart enough to have applied it my life. I'd like to tell you I was smart enough not to go back and do the same stuff shuffle. Unfortunately, I'd be lying. I repeated this exercise in futility a few times over the coming weeks as I tried to declutter the entire kitchen or all the kids' toys in one sitting. Invariably, I'd make a little progress but a whole lot more mess and would feel inadequate and more frustrated than when I'd begun.

Do you know the best way to eat an elephant? A fairly disgusting question, really, but there's wisdom in the answer: one bite at a time.

I'd been trying to swallow the whole damn elephant for weeks and wondering why I kept choking.

I'm a slow study; it takes me a long time to learn new things. In fact, when I was sixteen and learning to drive, I found it impossible to reverse a car with any confidence. I never knew which way the wheel was supposed to turn in order to get the car to move the way I wanted it to. Something about the process of flipping directions and making things work backward was stupidly difficult. My friends used to stand in front of my car as I was reversing out of a parking spot at school, my mom in the passenger seat, and they'd spin an imaginary steering wheel in front of their bodies to show me which direction to turn the wheel. Of course, being sixteen, they thought it was very funny to encourage me to turn it the wrong way, which resulted in much hilarity (for them) and confusion (for me). This went on for longer than I'm willing to admit.

Starting Small

Despite my slow learning, I eventually arrived at the realization that I'd been coming at decluttering from the wrong perspective. Instead of thinking about the elephant as a massive meal to be completed in one sitting, I needed to think of it as a year-long feast made up of tiny little bites. (You know what? I'm just going to say it. Here ends the elephant as a meal analogy.)

I needed to flip my thinking on decluttering and remove some of the urgency I'd attached to it. I was operating on a tight deadline, but I was the only one who knew about it, because I was the one who'd created it.

So I decided to go to the opposite end of the spectrum and start small. Like, really, really small.

I cleaned out my handbag first. Endless receipts and pens and the varied detritus of two young kids emerged, and as I let go of every handful and hung my now completely clutter-free handbag on the hook behind our front door, I felt a relief I hadn't experienced in any of my bigger, partially successful decluttering efforts.

Next, I cleaned out the front two seats of our car. Mail and catalogs were recycled, and empty drink bottles and tissue boxes and toys were removed and recycled or thrown away. The back seat of the car followed, which unearthed more crumbs than I'd thought possible and enough Happy Meal toys to make me distinctly uncomfortable.

After the car, I decluttered just one drawer in the kitchen. Not the whole kitchen, as I'd tried previously, but just one drawer. Again, I felt a physical sensation of relief with each utensil I put in a bag, bound for the secondhand shop. I hadn't realized an excess of spatulas and wooden spoons could impact my well-being, but the lightness I felt when I dropped the bag off told me otherwise.

Finally, I'd discovered the key to sustainable simplifying: time. Part of that was because I had very young kids and limited hours in which I could sort through our stuff, but mostly it was to avoid the crushing sense of exhaustion I faced every time I tried to tackle a big job. Too many decisions, too many emotions, too much sentimentality, and

How I imagined simplifying

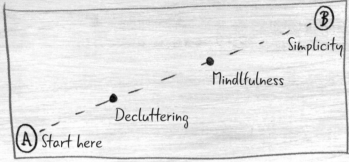

Ⓑ Simplicity

Mindlfulness

Decluttering

Ⓐ Start here

The reality

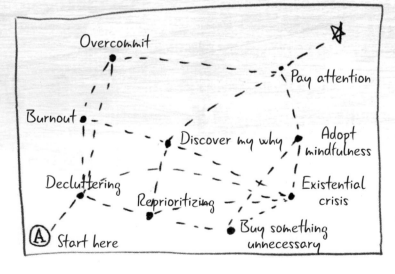

Overcommit

Pay attention

Burnout

Discover my why

Adopt mindfulness

Decluttering

Reprioritizing

Existential crisis

Ⓐ Start here

Buy something unnecessary

too many what-ifs waited in the boxes in our garage, but one drawer? I could do that. So I did. Over and over and over again.

Over a period of weeks, I worked through the rest of the kitchen drawers, one at a time. I moved on to the medicine cabinet and decluttered each shelf in there, one at a time. Similarly, with the bathroom vanities, I broke the task down into manageable chunks by committing to only one drawer or one shelf at a time. If I felt like doing more, great, but breaking it down into those bite-sized pieces meant the pressure was gone and the heavy feeling of overload all but disappeared.

I then gradually moved through our bookshelves and storage containers, our linen closet, and bedside tables in much the same way, until one day, I realized I'd decluttered much more than I ever expected to.

There was a lightness to me I hadn't experienced before as I began to see the benefits of this slow, sustainable work. There was a little more white space in our home—somewhere for my eye to rest that wasn't overwhelmed by stuff. There was less tidying to do, less dusting and picking up and stacking and ordering and organizing, which meant I had more time than I'd had previously. All from these small, almost insignificant steps. These were some of the small jobs I tackled:

- handbag
- wallet/purse

- car
- glove compartment

- utensils drawer
- junk drawer
- medicine cabinet
- corner of the kitchen bench
- front of the fridge
- top of the fridge
- coat rack
- toiletries in the shower or bath
- makeup and cosmetics
- Tupperware drawer

The biggest surprise of all was that I felt energized to do more. Suddenly, the specter of the garage wasn't as terrifying. The idea of simplifying my bulging wardrobe wasn't making me anxious, and the notion of working through the kids' toys made me excited rather than daunted. The benefits were now solidly outweighing the work involved, and the lightness I felt was well worth the effort required to get there.

I also became more confident in making decisions on what to keep and what to let go of, because there was literally nothing I missed. In fact, it was difficult to even recall what I'd let go of over the past weeks. That's how insignificant the stuff was in comparison to the feeling of not having it.

After that, the work of big decluttering jobs happened with more ease. I worked through the kids' toys, and they were each left with enough as opposed to an overstimulating level of too much. I turned my attention to my wardrobe and let go of dozens (and dozens) of items that didn't fit or didn't make me feel good. An embarrassing

number of shoes were carted off to the secondhand shop, along with multiple pairs of jeans.

Even decluttering the previously overwhelming garage was an easier task. Over a few weeks, we were able to empty the garage of the boxes—most of the contents were sold in two garage sales over that summer, and whatever didn't sell went straight to the secondhand shop. One afternoon, Ben and I found ourselves sitting in the backyard, looking at the now-empty double garage that took up so much space, and made another decision—we no longer needed the garage.

We sold the entire building structure to a neighbor's friend, tore up the concrete slab, and replaced it with grass, a trampoline, and a vegetable garden. I now watch my kids play in that space every single day and couldn't find an example that better represents how much we stand to gain when we choose to let go. That space used to be full of stuff—heavy, unimportant, but ever-present. Now, it's a space for family, play, gardening, growth, and life. It's a space we all love, and it came from letting go of what we didn't need.

Steps Toward a Slower Life

Despite everything I've just written, I'm actually really hesitant to closely align the idea of decluttering with the philosophy of slow living, because they're not the same thing. Slowing down and simplifying aren't centered solely on the idea of decluttering, but letting go of excess is an important part of slowing down.

Minimalism is often tied to slow living, and while they are a wonderful complement to each other and I personally tend to a more minimalist aesthetic, they also aren't the same thing. At its core, minimalism is about stripping out excess stuff in order to make room for the things that matter, but it so often becomes twisted around the competitive idea of how much we should own, how many items we can live with, how bare the walls are, how tiny the home, how tightly edited the capsule wardrobe. All these things can be part of a slow, simple life, but I find so many people get overwhelmed at the idea of "doing minimalism right" that we essentially swap the old Joneses for new.

The new Joneses seem to have conflated the minimalist aesthetic with minimalism as a lifestyle (they are very different things). Their homes look like something straight out of a magazine spread and are simply another brand of unachievable status. So we find ourselves comparing our lives with a new set of icons. We wonder whether our level of stuff is enough or perhaps still too much. Too busy. Too boring.

Instead, think of decluttering as one step in the process of creating a slower, simpler life, not the goal. It's more about approaching our home—and the things we choose to keep in it—with intention. It's about choosing actively what things to hold on to, what things to let go of, and what things are meaningful to us. There is no right or wrong, but we do have a choice.

By giving ourselves physical space, we're providing buffer and margin and room to breathe. Less stuff means less maintenance, less dusting, less tidying, fewer decisions, less stress. Removing the excess means more space, more time, more opportunity for things that fill us up.

I never realized how heavy my stuff was until I didn't have to carry it around anymore. Every carload that went to the secondhand shop, every garage sale, every load of recycling was a weight off my shoulders I hadn't realized was there. And if you're skeptical, I don't blame you. So many people I speak with feel the same way. How can our things impact us so dramatically?

Clutter is deferred decisions. It's the physical manifestation of procrastination. It's overcommitment in the form of stuff. And if you consider how you feel when there is a project looming at work or an assignment deadline on the horizon and you can't make yourself act on it, that low-level anxiety, that pang in the gut is the feeling a lot of our clutter brings.

Americans spend more than $32 billion on external storage every year, and while sometimes people use the space to store things like wine collections, excess stock, important documents, or personal belongings while moving or traveling, many of these storage units are filled with excess *stuff*, such as furniture, homewares, and sentimental items that have been set aside and forgotten. If you can imagine what a storage unit full of your unwanted excess might look like and expand that out to an entire country's worth of clutter… That's a lot of stuff weighing down a lot of people.

Even in our own homes, we buy storage solutions for stuff we don't look at. We put it in the garage, shed, attic, or basement, and we pretend it's not there. We spring-clean and find a little breathing room once a year, and we spend the following twelve months slowly replacing the stuff we let go of, only to find ourselves repeating the process the following spring. It's a cycle that won't be broken unless we ask the uncomfortable questions, examine our relationship with stuff, and accept that we have a choice in how our homes make us feel.

I won't pretend this is an easy thing to do. It's not. Decluttering is tiring and repetitive, and it brings us face-to-face with a lot of thoughts and feelings we've tried to bury underneath our stuff. It can be uncomfortable, physically and emotionally, but it's also not rocket science. In her 2012 book, *Tiny Beautiful Things: Advice on Love and Life from Dear Sugar*, Cheryl Strayed was asked how to overcome the difficult nature of writing (to which, right at this very moment, I can personally attest). She replied, "Writing is hard for every last one of us… Coal mining is harder. Do you think miners stand around all day talking about how hard it is to mine for coal? They do not. They simply dig." So simply dig. Do the work of sorting, deciding, and letting go, and do a little bit of it every single day. I guarantee you will dig deeper and go further by doing this daily than if you waited for inspiration to strike and tried to tackle your clutter in one go.

But what if you can't move forward even a little bit? What if digging simply becomes too difficult to face?

First, there is always something you can do to move forward, a tiny action that will improve your current position. Pick up one piece of paper, and put it in the recycling bin. Find one pen that no longer works, and throw it away. Remove one book or magazine from the bookshelf, and acknowledge that a tiny step forward is still a step forward. Second, I've come to realize that many of the obstacles I faced when decluttering—loss of identity, resistance, sentimentality, the amount of money spent—are super common, and I wanted to address them here. Being able to identify these issues and acknowledging there are ways to move through or around them means the obstacle won't stop you from progressing. Imperfect action is still action, after all.

The Six Obstacles to Decluttering

FEAR

After I chose to discontinue my jewelry label, I spent many months in limbo. I didn't want to go back, but I couldn't move forward either, because I was terrified. I'd left hundreds of pieces of jewelry in my abandoned studio, and I was unable to even look at them, because they made me feel sick, but I also couldn't consider letting them go. My identity for the past few years had been tied directly to that jewelry, and to give it away was admitting I wasn't the person I thought I was. I wasn't the go-get-'em budding entrepreneur or the hard worker or the mom who managed to balance work and stay-at-home parenting, and what did that say about me? Those questions and realizations were painful, and I avoided them for as long as possible, so the clutter remained, hidden from view but still very much present.

Fear can take many forms as you work through this process—some obvious and others more insidious. We're afraid of forgetting, of what happens next, of getting older and becoming irrelevant, so we hold on. We fear the loss of identity that comes from realizing we're no longer the crafty person or the snowboarder, the suit-wearing corporate or the comic-book collector, so we keep the things that tie us to that story, afraid to look too closely lest we see how much we've changed.

When we hold on to stuff we no longer need, use, or even want, we're choosing one form of discomfort over another. We're choosing to remain stuck, cluttered, and overwhelmed instead of asking the difficult questions or acknowledging the fact that we have changed and time has moved on. The biggest difference between those two forms of discomfort is that positive change lies on the other side of only one of them.

I eventually gave away all that jewelry, because I'd realized that, while it sat in my studio, it was holding me back. I continued to tie my identity to this stuff, but instead of being a positive thing, it had morphed into self-loathing and failure. Why would I want to keep that around? Letting go of it was both a physical release and a liberation. Plus, it was actually far less scary and far more exhilarating than I'd imagined. Once I'd acknowledged change and removed my judgment of it—time is passing regardless—I was able to let go. Just like that. The dam burst, and I found I could let go of so much more stuff and so many more stories, gradually allowing myself to build the life I wanted *now* rather than the one I'd thought I wanted years ago.

If you find yourself afraid of what might be revealed once you let go of the things that are no longer relevant to you, try to reframe your fear. By letting go of the paints you no longer use, the comic books you no longer collect, the guitar you no longer play, the snowboard you bought in a fit of enthusiasm but have only ridden once in six years, you reveal different parts of yourself. You're giving yourself the opportunity to

We hold off decluttering out of fear, shame, guilt, expectations. We avoid letting go because of the money already spent, the previous memories attached to things, the terror when we realize time is passing and there's nothing we can do to stop it. We cling on to things in the fuzzy belief we will need them again someday—even if that someday is decades in the making—or because we don't want our stuff to be thrown in landfill but have no idea what else to do with it. But these obstacles present us with an opportunity to move forward and let go, if only we allow it.

grow and explore and try new things and think in different ways, and it's incredibly liberating.

EXTERNAL RESISTANCE

When I first began decluttering, I wanted to blame our excess on the kids. There were toys and play sets and teddy bears and endless amounts of tiny clothes. Not to mention bibs and wraps and blankets and pacifiers. Focusing on things that weren't mine and couldn't possibly be my fault meant I moved through the process with a moral superiority that was unearned. When I examined the bigger picture, the majority of things that cluttered up our garage, our bedrooms, our shed, and the "office" (a.k.a. the junk room) weren't the kids' things but mine. And I didn't much like admitting that.

I'm so often asked what to do if a partner, kids, friends, or family aren't on board with decluttering. What if they like clutter? What if they don't want to let go of their excess stuff? This is a super valid concern and can be a big stumbling block, but it's also a great excuse for us to do nothing.

We are so inclined to procrastination, to looking hard for a reason not to do the thing we know we need to do, that when faced with the challenge of decluttering, it's very easy to let other people's stuff become that reason. I'd encourage you to look inward, dealing with your own clutter and your own hang-ups first. You might be surprised at just how much of the decision making is in your hands, and once the stuff has gone, things might feel a whole lot more manageable.

By choosing to live a simpler life, even a compromised version of it, you will be leading by example. Rather than telling your partner or kids about decluttering and its benefits, show them. Work through your home, space by space, room by room, removing all the clutter that belongs to you. If there are shared areas or things that belong to the entire family, leave those for now. Just focus on the things *you* own. Clothes, shoes, books, CDs, DVDs, makeup or toiletries, craft or hobby items, photos, and keepsakes from your past—these are all things you can work through without impacting anyone else. Start there.

As the benefits of simplifying those areas become apparent—more space and less cleaning are two benefits that are very attractive to a lot of people—your family may just start paying attention. As you continue to work through your things, avoid the temptation to evangelize, and simply enjoy the benefits.

I've heard countless stories from people who started with a lot of resistance from a partner, and this gentle introduction to simplifying had much greater impact than the previous nagging ever did. Plus, no one enjoys being the shrew, so take that hat off, and start looking after the actions you can control—your own.

The flip side of that, however, is to be reasonable in your expectations of your partner. People have differing ideas about what constitutes clutter, what is meaningful, and what is beautiful. Part of sharing a home with someone is an openness to a certain level of compromise. Remember, the reason you're slowing down and simplifying is to make life better, so don't add a whole heap of stress to the equation unnecessarily.

INTERNAL RESISTANCE

Decluttering will deliver many powerful moments of realization, freedom, and liberation, and for me, the internal resistance has been heaviest just before those breakthroughs.

If you find yourself completely stuck, unable to declutter for no discernible reason, you could be on the verge of a big breakthrough. Conversely, you could also be on the verge of overload. When you feel yourself getting stuck, check in and ask why you're feeling like that— are you afraid of what might come next? Or are you paralyzed by the enormity of the job you've undertaken?

If it's the former, check in with your Why. Revisit the reasons for doing this work in the first place and what you stand to gain by doing it. Checking in with your Why is so powerful and usually enough of a motivator to get you moving forward again—even if it's only in a very small way.

In the case of sheer overload, you might simply have gone in too big. You might have lost sight of the small steps that exist between today

The feeling of lightness that
comes from having less is
often the best persuasion.

and tomorrow, instead focusing on a year from now. It's motivating and exciting to think about the long-term destination, but it can also leave us feeling defeated by the work we have in front of us. We can't see all the steps between here and there, but if we focus on the single step in front of us, everything becomes much simpler, because we only need to take that next step. Once we've taken it, the following step reveals itself, and we can then take it in turn. Have a little faith in the process, keep taking your small steps every day, and trust that the breakthroughs, freedom, and clarity will come. Not necessarily every day (or even every week!), but they will come.

The third possibility is that you're just tired. So give yourself a break. Making these changes is hard work, and it's totally normal to feel the effects of that. If that's the case, see if there's a tiny task you can do—pick up one thing that's out of place and return it, wipe the kitchen counter-top, file one piece of paper—then go and do something completely unrelated to simplifying. Take a walk, have a cup of tea in the sunshine, read a book, listen to music, play with your kids, do something creative. This is the golden stuff of life. Sometimes you need to fill yourself up again before getting back to work.

SENTIMENTALITY

The notion of sentimentality is a big, important one, but it also acts as a catchall excuse for us not to get started in the first place. While there are many reasons people attach emotional importance to things, not all of them are valid or useful. The best place to begin when you hear yourself saying that an item is of sentimental value is to ask yourself if that's actually true.

Is the item really of sentimental importance, or are you just telling yourself that in order to not have to act? Is the item itself important? Or is it the memory attached to it? I admit to not being an overly sentimental person, which means this is a slightly easier area to navigate for me, and I haven't suffered the loss of a parent, child, or partner, so my relationship with stuff hasn't been further complicated in that way. However, I've spoken with countless people who are either hugely sentimental or have suffered a loss—or both—and in every instance, learning to let go was a healing process for them too. It almost invariably takes longer to let go, but the outcome is similarly freeing.

For me, it's been important to recognize that the place, time, memory, person, or relationship does not exist *in* the item. The item is simply a shape made of glass or a combination of fabrics. It's a cup or a bowl or a piece of furniture that reminds us of a time that's passed, and we can start to remove the emotion from the item by viewing it a little more dispassionately.

As always, there is no right or wrong. What matters is intention. If you take the time to truly question your reason for holding on to these items and you're happy to do so, then you've achieved intention.

If you find yourself struggling to let go of sentimental items, asking yourself the following three questions can help:

1. Does this item actually mean something to me?

    Often, we keep things because we think we should or because the item is representative of good times, fun vacations, our now-grown children, or people we love. But does the actual item, the thing you're holding in your hand, mean something to you? If not (and you may be surprised by how many of these things do not mean anything on close inspection), then the decision to remove it from your home should be simple. Decide whether to donate, recycle, or throw it away.

2. What emotion does this item represent?

    Study that emotion for a moment.

    What is it? Why do you feel it?

    Would you still feel that emotion without the physical item? If yes, then your decision has again been made.

    Do you have multiple items that rouse the same emotion?

    What if you kept one or two things that are truly meaningful and representative of that emotion instead of blindly keeping everything that's related to the person, time, or place?

If there is no strong emotional attachment, then you can more easily decide to remove the item from your home.

3. Would I display the item in my home?

We all keep things we wouldn't display in our home, and you don't need to remove everything that you wouldn't hang on the wall, but asking yourself this question forces you to really examine why you're holding on to the item and what the item itself means to you.

If you wouldn't display it, then really question your reasons for keeping it. Remember, there is no right or wrong here; the intention is to pare down and simplify these sentimental things.

Once you've asked yourself these questions and decided whether to keep the item, donate it, recycle it, or throw it away, you can let go and be proud.

MONEY SPENT

One of the biggest obstacles to letting go is the money we see in our stuff. The hobbies we never pursued, the sports we never really enjoyed, the clothes we never quite fit into after having kids. In these items, we see shame, wastefulness, money not well spent, and if we let them go, it means that money has been wasted.

Unfortunately, that money is already gone. Now you're stuck with a thing you don't use as well as the guilt associated with not actually using it. Forgive yourself and let it go. You will regain space, both physical and emotional, and you'll also start paying closer attention to the things you invite or allow into your house.

JUST IN CASE

We hold on to things just in case we're going to need them later. But when we take that thought process to its logical end, most "just in case" reasons are kind of ridiculous.

I'll keep these five surplus spatulas just in case. Just in case I'm cooking five batches of pancakes at once? Just in case this one spatula that I use every single time suddenly becomes unattractive to me? Just in case I lose my spatula and all the stores no longer sell them?

I'll keep this book I've read and didn't enjoy just in case. Just in case it turns out to be a classic? Just in case the plot holes, horrible characters, or preachy tone stop being annoying? Just in case someone else wants to read it? They can of course—at the library.

I'll hold on to these pants from high school just in case. Just in case I lose the weight I've been carrying for the past five years? Just in case the style comes back in fashion? Just in case I need these specific pants for a costume party?

I'll hold on to every single artwork my kids have ever created just in case. Just in case they want to sort through twelve plastic boxes full of finger-painting and high school essays when they move into their own home? Just in case they become brilliant artists and want to see how far they've come? Just in case they want to use it all to start a bonfire?

Once you realize what you're actually saying, it becomes clear that "just in case" is simply another way we try to put off decision making. Instead, take control of the things you allow into your home and the things that get a piece of your attention. Extra spatulas and too-small pants don't really qualify.

Where to Get Rid of the Excess Stuff

One of the common reasons people choose to embrace a slower life stems from a concern for our environment. We know we need to be better stewards of the planet, so it makes sense that one of the biggest obstacles people have when it comes to decluttering is what to do with the excess we no longer want. Maybe we want to recoup our money or give things to different charities. Maybe we'd like to give our clutter away to friends or family or see items upcycled into something beautiful. So much of our excess is still completely fine and usable. Surely there are better things to do with it than tossing it into landfill and condemning those resources to literally rot in the ground?

The simplest way to declutter and minimize harm is to just give your

Let go of the guilt of removing the item from your home. Let go of the weight of the thing you are keeping. Be proud that you are surrounding yourself with things that are truly meaningful.

stuff away. My preferred way to do this is to choose one charity and let it benefit from your excess. However, it can get complicated or frustrating if that charity won't accept a certain type of item; increasingly books, furniture, and electrical goods are being turned away due to excess supply or safety concerns. You can explore other ways to donate your goods via Freecycle or buy-swap-sell groups on Facebook, and there are many local services that could benefit too. Local playgroups and preschools may want your excess toys or kitchenware; refugee centers, women's shelters, veterans' charities, or nursing homes could be in need of clothing, furniture, toys, books, and magazines. The local library, community garden, or neighborhood center may appreciate donations too, or perhaps there is a communal garage sale that could raise funds by selling your stuff. A little bit of research, a few phone calls, and you will find a number of ways to put your unwanted stuff to good use, extending its life for many years to come.

If you want to sell your items and recoup some of the money, no worries, but give yourself a deadline. If it hasn't sold (on eBay or at your garage sale, for example) by the time that deadline passes, give that stuff away.

If you have grand plans to repair, upcycle, or reuse your excess stuff, that's fantastic. Similarly, give yourself a deadline to finish the project, and if you don't get around to it within that time frame, pass it on.

Composting and recycling are good options for things that can't be donated, sold, or reused, and they are far preferable to throwing items in the garbage. Of course, not everything can be recycled or composted, so be sure to check what materials will be accepted in your curbside recycling program, or ask your local municipality if they have regular programs for recycling items such as mattresses, computers, old electrical goods, or printer cartridges. You can usually recycle old phones at the store you bought them from, and many tech stores will take your old computers or laptops and refurbish them for use in schools or low-cost programs for people who couldn't otherwise access technology.

Whatever you choose to do with your excess, simply act. Because that broken plastic toy isn't going to become less broken or less plastic by sitting in the garage for six months. Similarly, the smartphone that no longer works or the shoes that are too old to be reheeled are not going to become useful if you wait. Don't let this become a roadblock to your simplifying.

You will probably feel a lot of guilt about this excess—particularly the stuff that can't be donated, upcycled, or reused—but use that guilt as an opportunity to commit to making better choices going forward, buying only what you need, making sure the materials will last and can be composted or recycled at the end of their usefulness, and move on as best you can.

How to Declutter

There are many ways of approaching the actual work of decluttering. Marie Kondo, in her worldwide bestselling book *The Life-Changing Magic of Tidying Up*, advocates for a big, category-specific style of decluttering. For example, get all your books out and put them somewhere central, work through every one in a single session, letting go of those that aren't used or don't "spark joy." This is an approach that's worked incredibly well for millions of people worldwide, and I think the question of whether something sparks joy is beautiful and practical, allowing for the fact that sometimes our belongings really do bring us joy.

For others, as you've seen from my story, that approach can be a direct route to Overload Town, and perhaps unsurprisingly, as an advocate of small, consistent action, I'd encourage you to go small first and move on to bigger tasks as your confidence builds.

There is no one right way of letting go of your excess, and regardless of which approach you take, please know that the decluttering process will almost certainly be repeated more than once, because it takes time to recalibrate and find your level of enough. We worked through every part of our home at least three times before we felt like the majority of the clutter was gone, and I still regularly question what can stay and what we no longer have a need for. I don't tell you this to discourage you but rather to encourage you to take imperfect action anyway. No, you probably won't nail it straight out of the gate, and that's fine. That's great, actually. Start anyway.

Choose an area of your home to declutter—based on where it's needed most or whatever feels manageable to you right now—then choose a very small part of that area. That might mean one drawer in the kitchen, one shelf in the bathroom, one end of the kitchen counter, or one pile of papers in the office, but if that feels too big or overwhelming, break it down further. One corner of the shelf, ten items in the drawer, or half a pile of papers. The key is to make it as easy as possible to get started. Small steps taken consistently will see you make more progress over time than the occasional big push, even if they feel insignificant in the beginning.

Once you've decided on the space you'll be decluttering, remove everything from that space and put it on a clear surface nearby.

Wipe down your now-empty shelf/drawer/corner/table (I use either a water and white vinegar mix or water with a few drops of tea tree or lavender oil in a spray bottle). Not only does it clean the surface you're working on, but the symbolic idea of a new start shouldn't be underestimated either.

Ethical decluttering

(before you throw away your unwanted stuff,
can you do any of these instead?)

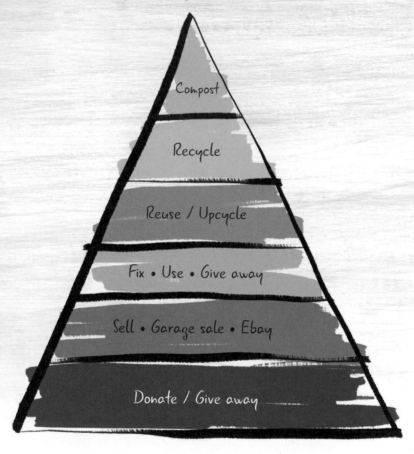

Compost

Recycle

Reuse / Upcycle

Fix • Use • Give away

Sell • Garage sale • Ebay

Donate / Give away

Start at the bottom—these are the most
sustainable and uncomplicated options.

Grab a handful of empty shopping bags or boxes and nominate one as the donate bag, one for recycling, and one for garbage. Then start by simply picking up one item and asking yourself:

- Do I want this?
- Do I like it?
- Do I need this?
- Do I have multiples of the same thing?
- How many of this thing do I really need?
- Do I have another item that can do the same job?
- Do I use this?
- How often do I use it?
- Can I do without it?
- Do I want to do without it?
- If I don't use it very often, can I borrow or rent it when I do need it?

Based on your answers, choose where the item goes. If you're keeping it, put it back in its place; if you're going to donate, recycle, or throw it out, put it in the correct bag and move on to the next item. The key is to deal with one thing at a time and not move on until you've decided what to do with it.

Obviously, not every item will require a deep dive on its usefulness.

Some things you will pick up and immediately think, "Why do I still have this?" Some things will be immediate keepers, and others will take a slightly deeper questioning.

Don't overcomplicate it. Your first response is usually the best one to go with, and being happy with your decision is important. It's about being intentional—that is, keeping things on purpose and letting things go with the same level of choice.

Once you've worked through everything that was in the space to be decluttered, deal with the piles by recycling all you can immediately, throwing away anything broken or unsalvageable, and packing up everything you'd like to give away. Once the donate bag is full, put it near the front door or in the back of your car, and drop it into your local charity bin the next time you're out. Chances are you're going to make that trip a lot over the coming months, and every single trip will represent a further lightening.

This basic approach for decluttering is going to see you through most of the simplifying that lies ahead. Those basic questions will help you recognize what is and isn't important, what you do and don't need, and what you actually use versus what you're told you should be using, and they're also going to help you recognize the sheer volume of things we surround ourselves with.

There are a few strategies that can help simplify this process even more or help you move past some of the common obstacles on the road to a simpler home. I've found a combination of these strategies has been instrumental in moving through my own stumbling blocks or when I've found myself backsliding.

EXPERIMENT

You can't fail an experiment, which is why this is one of the best ways to approach difficult situations or let go of sticky clutter. It's a really fun opportunity to ask ourselves "What would happen if…" and create a set of circumstances that allow us to play around with the idea, with very little risk.

We recently had the inside of our house painted, which meant all our artwork, photos, and kids' craft projects had to come off the walls. Once the painting was completed, we decided to leave the walls empty for a week and see how we felt. The week stretched to a month, and we still hadn't put anything on the walls, because both Ben and I quite liked the peacefulness of white space in each room.

It wasn't until we had a lot of wet weather that we both got frustrated at the lack of coat hooks behind our front door, and after a while, we missed the injection of personality the kids' art wall brought to our living room. So their artwork went back up when the coat hooks did. We also felt the absence of a few favorite pieces of art and our massive world map, so they were eventually returned to their original places. The difference was that they weren't hung because we thought we should or that it would be weird for us not to. They were hung because we wanted them there and because those things are part of the home we want, not the home we think we should have.

Experiment by removing the artwork from a room in your home or putting all the barely used toys in a few boxes in the shed, and wait to see if anyone misses them. Pack away sentimental items—books, kitchenware, souvenirs, and knickknacks—and simply see if you need, want, or miss them. By removing them from use and only getting things out if they're needed, you get a good sense of what really is important as opposed to what we tell ourselves is important. And the difference between the two is often huge.

Another really simple one to try is the clothes hanger experiment. At the beginning of the season, turn all your clothes hangers around so they're facing the opposite direction. As you wear, wash, and put the item back in your wardrobe, turn the hanger around so you can tell that the item's been worn. Over the season, you'll get a clear picture of the clothes you actually wear as opposed to the clothes you keep for other reasons. This makes it so much easier to let go at the end of the season as you can clearly identify what hasn't been worn.

CHECK IN WITH YOUR WHY

If you find yourself getting bogged down in the tiny decisions or the insignificant items, take a look at why you're here. Why are you working so hard to slow down and simplify? What are you looking to gain? Checking in with that list of eulogy-worthy items will help you find perspective in the decision making and also help you recognize that so much of what we agonize over in the moment simply isn't important. If you're struggling to let go of the sentimental or the sticky, a good dose of perspective might just be enough of a boost.

RULES AND BOUNDARIES

Rules are made to be broken, and boundaries are just asking to be pushed, but having a few of each in your home can make it so much easier to keep a lid on the gradual buildup of sneaky clutter.

"One in, one out" is a great place to begin. If you bring something new into your home—clothes, decor, toys—then you need to remove at least one thing to make space for it, which not only helps keep your stuff to a manageable amount but forces you to question whether you're willing to let go of something just so you can bring a new thing in.

If you have a tendency to collect things (maybe shoes, DVDs, comics, books, Star Wars figurines, LEGO, wooden trains, skateboards, stones, or pretty papers), then nominate an area for those things and don't let them exceed that space. For example, our kids have a limited amount of space for their toys (a toy box under their beds and a small bookshelf in their bedrooms) and once their toys start to expand beyond those boundaries, they know it's time to go through their collection and let go of the ones they no longer need or want.

The same applies to other areas of the home—the kitchen, for example. If you only have space for eight wineglasses, then keep eight wineglasses. If you want to buy new wineglasses, you'll need to free up room by giving away the others.

If you have a small closet, you'll need to be mindful about what you wear, what you keep, how each item works with other items you own, and whether there's something in there that can be removed if you bring a new piece of clothing home.

This is one of the biggest benefits of having tight boundaries—it keeps us mindful of what we allow into our homes.

○ ○ ○

Before I move on to the next chapter and begin looking at how to minimize our consumption and rethink our ideas of ownership, I have to be honest. I was hesitant to include this chapter, because over the years, I've come to realize that none of this is about things at all. Nothing about life is the stuff we accumulate. It's the people, the memories, the kindness, the relationships.

And yet there is a real *need* for this chapter on decluttering, because we are still overwhelmed with stuff. We still hold onto our excess out of fear or obligation. We still buy things to fill a gap in our life. We still use our things to identify the kind of person we are. And it's all become too much. We've gone above need, beyond enough, and we've moved into excess.

I don't want slow living to become synonymous with decluttering, but I do want it to become synonymous with intention. And if you can work through the process of decluttering with intention, then you can feel confident that a slower, simpler home waits on the other side.

How much time
and/or energy
do you have for decluttering right now?

Honestly not much
Like, maybe five or ten minutes, max.

- purse
- wallet
- handbag
- coat rack
- empties in the shower
- diaper bag
- takeout menus

- pens that don't work
- under the kitchen sink
- sock drawer
- front seat of car
- back seat of car
- car trunk

- car glove box
- junk mail
- expired makeup
- bedside table
- the top of the fridge

- cutlery drawer
- medicine cabinet
- vanity
- toiletries
- one junk drawer
- shoes
- utensils drawer

- towels
- sheets
- pantry
- magazine pile
- fridge
- underwear drawer
- coffee table

- dining table
- glassware
- crockery
- Tupperware drawer (and lids)
- gym gear

I am ready

to face my destiny. Let me prove myself.

- wardrobe
- kids' toys
- boxes in garage
- shelves in garage
- attic—boxes
- attic—other

- garden shed
- basement
- baby items
- tops of wardrobes
- CD collection

- bookshelves
- sentimental items—boxes
- photo albums
- DVDs

three

DE-OWN

I always wanted to work in the film industry. Not in front of the camera (good lord, no), but as a screenwriter. So when my first job after college was as a receptionist in a busy postproduction film house at a studio in Sydney, I was on my way. I sat in (eavesdropped) on script meetings with a Hollywood director, watched as an editor became increasingly exhausted working to finish his feature film, photocopied and assembled scripts, and saw just how boring much of the work that goes in to our entertainment actually is. But I didn't care.

n the beginning at least, I was energized and excited by the creativity and the occasional celebrity sighting, but mostly I was enamored of the possibility that given the right exterior, the right jeans, hair, and attitude, I might just fit in with the cool, creative people who walked past my desk every day.

I was actually a fairly terrible receptionist who lacked the confidence and organizational skills to do anything more than a passable job, but I became obsessed with finding the right jeans, the right haircut, and the right accessories, convinced that once I'd found them, my confidence would miraculously appear, and I'd be happy. I spent my small weekly wage on clothes and makeup, getting up at 4:30 a.m. to make sure I looked like someone who deserved to be part of something cool. It was tiring, but I was adulting! I bought into the idea that success and personal value looked a certain way, and I couldn't understand why I kept arriving at my destination (Indigo skinny jeans! Platinum blond hair! Red lipstick!) only to see that the goalposts had moved (Distressed denim! Brunette tones! Nude lips!), and I was late to the party again. It was an unwinnable race, but I'd taken up the challenge and wouldn't rest until I made the finish line.

Twenty-one-year-old me would have been embarrassed (but wealthier) to learn that little over a decade into the future, status and stuff have become incredibly dull to me.

Not only am I bored by it, but I'm also tired. Tired of stuff being used to measure our success and the value we place on others. Tired of people running themselves ragged trying to keep up with the Joneses. Tired of the endless want-buy-want-upgrade mentality. I detest the fact that even a well-adjusted adult can spend time on Instagram swinging wildly from self-acceptance to self-flagellation (and I'm devastated to think what this is doing to impressionable kids). I'm saddened by the social conditioning and the comparisons and the crappy novelty gifts. Mostly, though, I'm tired of the idea that this is normal.

Much to the surprise of twenty-one-year-old me, I hate shopping and avoid it as much as humanly possible. Fashion trends mean little to me, and most of my clothes are either a few years old or secondhand. I no longer upgrade to the newest smartphone. Our kids don't have every trend-driven piece of plastic junk that gets marketed to them. Our kitchen doesn't have a heap of gadgets, and our bookshelves are a lot less crowded since we've become fans of the local library. But it wasn't always like that.

When Ben and I first decluttered, we did a fantastic job of recluttering almost immediately. We've made space! Great! Let's fill it *with better stuff*. Stuff we need. Stuff we've always wanted. Stuff we deserve. Stuff that will identify us as successful and thoughtful. Stuff that will tell others we're creative, mindful, and intelligent.

Why did we do this? Why did we declutter, only to spend the next few months slowly recluttering? Why were we convinced that we deserved shiny, fancy, new things? Why did we find it difficult to maintain the space we worked so hard to create? For us, it was a combination of:

- convenience
- ego
- expectation
- habit
- boredom
- discontent
- comparison
- advertising
- status
- aspiration
- identity
- insecurity

Sure, some of the new stuff was warranted as our family grew and our requirements changed. But so much of it was simply a response to our social conditioning and the stories we told ourselves about success and status. What we failed to do in the beginning was to stop caring so much.

I want to be very clear and tell you that we still buy and own and use and enjoy things. We spend many happy afternoons listening to albums on our record player, and we go camping, snowboarding, traveling, and bike riding. I'm a keen gardener, my husband plays guitar and video games, and our kids are into drawing and LEGO, and we have the gear those activities require—but none of it has been bought without intention, and all of it is experiential. That is, we do things with it. It's not simply bought for the sake of owning it or signaling to others the kind of people we are.

Learning to be mindful of what we allow in and limiting it to what we truly need has been a huge part of creating and maintaining a simpler, slower home. Before that, the space we created was reconquered by bargains, impulse purchases, freebies, junk mail, party favors, big bags of hand-me-downs, four of a thing when one was enough, hard garbage collection gems, unwanted and unneeded gifts... There were a multitude of ways unwanted stuff found its way back into our home. Perhaps not surprisingly, I discovered the best way to minimize this gradual creep of new stuff was to simply pay attention.

Our society and economy are built upon a strong foundation of consumption and a firm expectation that we will contribute, so much so that choosing to live with less stuff is viewed as countercultural. We pick up the crappy novelty present for the office Christmas party because that's what everyone else does. We hang things on the wall because the neighbors might think we're weird if they remain empty, devoid of photos or artwork or trendy wall hangings. We browse the sale racks at our big box stores because that's what we've always done, and we allow TV or social media to fuel the fire of discontent (I'll be happy when we book a vacation...the kitchen is updated... we put in a pool).

Clutter creep

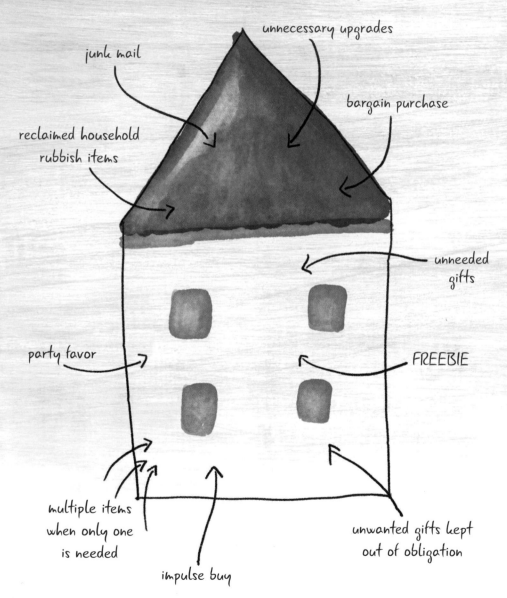

unnecessary upgrades

junk mail

bargain purchase

reclaimed household
rubbish items

unneeded
gifts

party favor

FREEBIE

multiple items
when only one
is needed

impulse buy

unwanted gifts kept
out of obligation

If we want change, we need to learn how to care less and how to care more. Care less about trends, status, and the outward signs of "success," and more about the important things. And we also need a good dose of gratitude.

Care Less by Embracing Perspective

There are billions of people in the world who *wish* their biggest issue was how to let go of the excess in their life. Instead, their concerns include shelter, food, water, and access to medical care for their families. They don't worry about having the right shade of lipstick, the correct boots, the newest iPhone, or the biggest TV screen but whether they will be safe going to sleep at night, or if the mosquitoes will make them sick, will the rain drip onto their infants, will there be food to eat tomorrow, will they get paid at the end of the week, is the spray they use on the crops making them cough...

I sit here, typing these words on my MacBook. I am clothed and fed and have access to clean water whenever I want it. If I cut my hand open while gardening later today, I can go to the hospital and have it stitched up. By doctors. In a clean facility. Tonight, I will flick a switch, and lights will turn on. I can make a phone call on the iPhone that is rarely more than ten feet from me.

It's sobering to realize the level of our privilege in the Western world and to see just how excessive our excess actually is. And while privilege is something I used to feel defensive about and ashamed of (How can I help where I was born? How is it my fault I've had opportunity while others haven't?), I now believe it's only something to be ashamed of if we don't do anything with it.

Because what is privilege if not opportunity? Opportunity to make things better for everyone? Opportunity to see inequity and rectify it? Opportunity to take these immense and lucky gifts and make them count toward a better world for those who didn't win the arbitrary where-you-were-born lottery?

I'm not going to hit you over the head with screams of "Privilege!" and "First world problems!" throughout this book, because the problem of too much *is* a real problem. Of course, some issues are bigger than others, but you're allowed to own your problems, not feel guilty about having them, and work toward solving them so you can start making choices that count for something more.

Perspective helps us to care less about the crap that doesn't matter and recognize how lucky we are that these are in fact our problems.

Care Less by Monitoring Your Inputs

We're exposed to more than three thousand marketing messages every day. What would happen if we started paying closer attention to the impact of these messages? What if we started questioning them a little more? What if we recognized that the main aim of these messages is not to make our lives better but to make us want to buy something? And not just things we need or even things we really want and will use, but things we're buying simply to fit in, to be on trend, to appear fashionable or knowledgeable.

Your eyeballs are being sold to the highest bidder, because entire industries depend on you being a mindless buyer. Don't be a mindless buyer. Pay attention to your inputs.

MAGAZINES

Start viewing the ads, editorials, and who wore it betters through a lens of skepticism. How often do we need a trashy, celebrity-filled magazine to tell us how to apply this month's hot makeup look? Or how to wear *the* high-waisted pants of the season? How many times do we need to be made to feel "less than" because of our age, body shape, gender, hair color, career opportunities, or fashion sense?

Glossy interiors magazines are the same, all hoping we'll buy into this vision of a successful life, a life where we get to be the Joneses— until, of course, a new set of Joneses comes along, with a bigger bathtub and more luxe kitchen countertops.

TV

When our kids were quite young, Ben and I made the intentional decision to not watch commercial TV. We watched public broadcast TV, Netflix, and DVDs. As a result, we watched a lot of really good programs, and as our kids moved through preschool and into school, they simply didn't know what the big, stupid trend in toys was that week.

Now school and YouTube bring their own exposure to trends, but there were five foundational years where the kids weren't conditioned to see an ad and want a thing, and it's held us in great stead as they've grown up. There is very little pestering to contend with and a whole lot more gratitude.

Consider cutting out or cutting back on commercial TV. Look at getting an on-demand streaming service instead of traditional cable or free-to-air, and limit the time spent flicking through commercial channels. Watching commercial TV quickly becomes unbearable as you begin to see just how many advertisements there are in a thirty-minute show (between eight and ten minutes of ad time, in case you were wondering) and how obtrusive they really are.

SOCIAL MEDIA

Who doesn't like a pretty picture or a glimpse into someone else's life/vacation/workspace? I enjoy Instagram as much as the next person, but like traditional media, you need to start viewing your social media channels through the same lens of skepticism.

Many wonderful, supportive, inclusive communities can be found online, and I wouldn't be writing this book if social media didn't exist, but so much of it is celebrity-soaked advertising dressed up as #authenticity.

Take a closer look at who you follow on social media and how their posts make you feel. If you're following them for travel inspiration or health tips and feel like you're learning or being inspired, that's great. But if you find yourself comparing homes, bodies, or wardrobes and walk away feeling inadequate, it's time to reconsider the impact their input is having on your life. So much of what is posited as authenticity is just another form of advertising. Social media celebrities can be paid as much as $10,000 to post a single photo of a product—regardless of whether they like it or use it.

Care Less by Embracing the Pause

If you feel yourself wanting to buy something…pause. When we pause, we give ourselves a moment in which to question our motivations. We can recognize a craving and then decide what to do with that craving (if anything). And if you establish some ways of building the pause into day-to-day life, you're giving yourself a buffer in which you can stop and ask why you now feel the need for something new.

The pause gives you an opportunity to really consider whether you want the thing and if it will have a positive or a negative impact on your life. This might mean creating a "buy it later" list, instigating a temporary spending ban, removing your credit card details from online store accounts, or taking shopping apps off your phone.

"Don't Just Declutter. De-own."

When I first read this instruction from Joshua Becker, author of *The More of Less* and creator of the blog *Becoming Minimalist*, I found it challenging. Decluttering and de-owning—aren't they the same thing? Isn't that what I had just worked my tail off doing? Decluttering our excess? De-owning it? Giving it away? Letting it go?

Now I can see that there's an important difference between decluttering our belongings and letting go of the need to own them at all, and I think this is one of the biggest lessons I had to learn. Previously, I'd found myself caught in the cycle of decluttering only to begin recluttering soon after as I succumbed to the pressure and expectations of what it meant to be an adult—someone who owns formal gowns and a good set of silverware. I've since discovered, however, that there are so many ways we can access the things we need without actually having

Don't be a mindless buyer. Share things. Borrow things. Rent things. Look after things. Fix things. Buy secondhand things. Buy once, and buy well. Buy ethically.

to buy them, and the rest of this chapter lists as many of these as possible. Keep in mind that these suggestions won't always be applicable to your situation, but embracing them where you can means the space you work hard to free up in your decluttering efforts will stay free.

SHARE THINGS

The sharing economy is growing at a rapid pace, and the idea of sharing resources is starting to take hold in the mainstream. In her 2012 TED talk, Rachel Botsman spoke of the sharing economy as a way to minimize buying things that have a limited use. Talking of handheld drills, which, on average, are used for a total of twelve to thirteen minutes throughout their entire life, she exclaimed, "You need the hole, not the drill!"

Turo, Lyft, TaskRabbit, and Airbnb are symbolic of the emergence of mainstream sharing, but there is a much more personal way to share that also taps into one of our most important resources—community.

Is there a way you and your family, friends, or neighbors could share common resources? Things you don't use very often but would probably go out and buy if the need arose? Perhaps one person could have extra wineglasses while another has the power drill? Someone else has the entertaining platters, and another has extra chairs or folding tables? Split a lawnmower between neighbors or share camping gear among friends?

For decades, there has been a box sitting on the table at my extended family gatherings. The box is ugly, beaten up, and scratched, and it's full of mismatched cutlery. My childhood memories are of barbecues and birthdays, Christmases and soup nights where the cutlery box sat on the table as countless hands dipped in and grabbed a fork or a dessertspoon. It went from house to house, helping to feed the people I love. No one cared that the cutlery didn't match. The box filled a need, and we were all free to use it if we had a party or an event at home.

Not only does sharing help you cut down on the things you need to buy, maintain, and store, but it is also a way of connecting with neighbors, friends, and family. In a small way, it reminds us that we're not alone, that we're part of something larger than ourselves.

Now, I am sure this is common sense to someone as lovely as you, but if you're going to go into an arrangement like this, don't be a jerk. Be generous with your lending, look after everything as if it were your own, and return it as soon as you've finished. (My parents may be reading this and scoffing at the thought of all the books of theirs I read and never returned over the years. Sorry, Pete and Bez. I'm better at it now! Plus, I go to the library instead.)

BORROW THINGS

I don't own a gravy boat. And while modern consumption and rules of adulting would have it that I should just go out and buy one, I choose to borrow one instead. My mother-in-law has a lovely gravy boat that she's more than happy to lend me on the annual occasion I might need one.

There is a stigma attached to borrowing things, however, and I think it's something we need to move beyond if we're to embrace slower, simpler living. We're told that real grown-ups own a power drill, a linen tablecloth, and ample wineglasses and that borrowing those things is a little bit lame, or inconvenient, or even intimidating. (Think of the people we might have to talk to! What if they say no?)

But having a conversation about borrowing offers us an opportunity to gain so much. I don't just mean a gravy boat or white tablecloth or some proper chardonnay glasses, but also relationships and connection and generosity. Being able to lend things to people and understand that your relationship is open to reciprocation is to create another layer of community. It's to admit, even in some small way, we don't have it all, and that's OK. It's letting down our guard and extending an invitation to others to join us in being a little more open and honest and generous.

There are things that don't lend themselves to easy borrowing, of course—toothpaste, pajamas, and irreplaceable sentimental items spring to mind (though I'd argue there are far less of those than we think)—but a little forethought and planning can open up a whole world of borrowing and lending that, in turn, frees up space in your home, reduces your footprint, and allows the opportunity for connection.

Things you can borrow from friends, family, or a close-knit crew of local people who are all happy to be part of a sharing circle include:

- suitcases
- sporting equipment—ski gear, surfboards, tennis rackets
- camping gear
- power tools
- extra blankets or bedding for occasional guests
- platters, crockery, and glassware
- cake tins
- books
- gardening equipment
- toys
- trailers
- cars
- kitchen appliances
- sewing machine
- baby gear
- lawnmower
- DVDs
- craft or hobby-related equipment

A significant part of slow living is learning to think intentionally and purposefully, and a little planning and forethought can go a long way. It's far more likely you'll rush out to buy the cake tin or extra sleeping bag if you've left it to the last minute. So think through events, trips, or dinner parties ahead of time and give yourself the opportunity to make the phone call or ask your friend at school drop-off.

Don't neglect more official methods of borrowing, such as from your local library. I will admit it took me a long time to come around to the idea of joining the library, as I was hooked on convenience. I wanted to read what I wanted, when I wanted it. So I spent a lot of money in bookstores, and I spent even more loading my iPad with ebooks from Amazon.

When my iPad took a graceful tumble down our back steps to the concrete below, I took it as a sign and visited the local library. Turns out I could preorder the books I wanted to borrow—online! I could keep a wish list of the titles I wanted to read! I could extend the borrowing time for up to six weeks! Where had this service been all my life? Oh, right. I'd ignored it simply because I thought it wasn't convenient enough.

More convenient, however, is saving money, resources, and space in our home by borrowing the dozens of books I read every year. And while I do still buy books, they're either ones I've borrowed at the library and know I will reread multiple times, secondhand novels that I sell back to our local secondhand bookstore when I'm done, reference books for work, or nonfiction titles that require a lot of scribbling, highlighting, and note-taking. I probably buy five new books a year now, as opposed to the dozens I used to buy.

Many local libraries also have the option to borrow movies, magazines, toys, DVDs, and other similar items, so be sure to check out the resources at your nearest branch.

RENT THINGS

Different from borrowing because there is an exchange of money, renting is still a great way of cutting back on ownership and reducing the money spent on single-use items.

When I have a fancy event to attend, such as a wedding, a ball, or an awards ceremony (and I say this like they happen all the time—which they definitely don't), I very rarely buy an outfit. Instead, I rent one.

I've been privy to some very interesting reactions when people realize I've rented my designer dress—anything from mild embarrassment to something resembling anger, as though I'm misleading people—but I figure that's more an issue for them than me. I not only save money by not needing to buy a dress, but I also get to wear some fun outfits I'd never have considered otherwise.

Of course, renting things doesn't stop at formal wear. You can rent:

- tools
- equipment
- catering supplies
- party needs
- decor
- indoor plants
- TVs
- fridges
- dishwashers
- computers
- A/V gear

- clothes
- accessories
- baby car seats
- bikes
- DVDs
- camping gear
- sporting equipment
- skis
- snowboards
- musical instruments
- furniture

No matter how much we simplify our homes, there will still be a need to own and purchase things. From everyday items to things we use on a semiregular basis, stuff like underwear, toiletries, clothes, shoes, a car or bike, computer, phone, camera, furniture, linen, kitchenware, and appliances are all things we will use and, to a certain extent, accumulate. The following suggestions are designed to help you minimize the need for new things, reduce the amount you spend on those things over time, and ensure that what you do bring into your home is going to have the most positive impact on your life—and your bank balance—as well as the people who make our things, and the planet we all share.

LOOK AFTER THINGS

Take care of the things you already own. Maintain the bike, polish the furniture, follow the laundry instructions, and take a little extra care. It costs a great deal less time and money to look after the things you already own than it does to replace them.

FIX THINGS

We have lost the art of repair. Clothes that could be mended by either ourselves or a seamstress are thrown away, a wobbly chair is more often than not relegated to the curbside pickup instead of being taken to a carpenter for repair, and it's usually cheaper to simply replace a broken electrical item than to have it fixed by a professional.

It might take some looking, but there are services that will fix your electrical items (search for repair shops in your local area), and I think it's time we rediscovered the skills of the cobbler, the seamstress, the furniture upholsterer, and the watchmaker. Your favorite pair of boots? Get them resoled. Your grandma's old chair? Try reupholstering it. The TV with the dodgy volume button? See if it can be repaired. Your old stove? It probably cooks as well as a modern one—get it serviced instead of replaced.

BUY SECONDHAND THINGS

A few years ago, I bought a pair of black leather motorcycle boots on eBay. I'd been wanting a pair for a long time but decided to see if I could find them secondhand. It took a few months, but eventually I found a pair I liked and paid a fraction of the price of buying new. The time and effort it took to find them secondhand has truly paid off, with the added benefit of less shopping and less expense. I still wear them every day in winter, and the high quality means I'll have them for years to come.

Chances are, everything you need already exists somewhere in the world. It's just a matter of finding it. As with so many of the strategies in this book, it simply requires a little forethought and patience.

Once you've found a style of jeans you love, why not scour eBay for your size? If you know your niece loves building timber train tracks, why not search your local secondhand and online stores for the few months leading up to her birthday? If you need a new dining table or a suitcase or a cowgirl costume, why not see how much of it can be bought secondhand before using more money and resources to buy new?

BUY ONCE, AND BUY WELL

Who hasn't felt the frustration of buying the cheap T-shirt, only to have it lose its shape within the first two washes? Or the poorly made flat-pack furniture that was fifty dollars cheaper but never quite fit together properly? Or the gardening tool that only cost five dollars but was covered in rust and unusable within a month?

If you do buy new, buy the best quality you can afford.

Obviously, price isn't a good indicator of quality—expensive doesn't necessarily mean quality, and cheap doesn't always mean poorly made—and it takes time to understand what quality looks like. But that is time worth spending, as it will save money and resources in the future.

Take a minute to feel the fabric or construction of the garment you're considering buying. Is it well put together? Are the seams reinforced? The jacket lined? The construction solid?

Look for online reviews. If the item you're looking at is a dud, you're sure to find hundreds of reviews telling you why. Check to see how long the item lasts or if there are any design flaws, then see if there's an alternative that might last longer or prove more durable. The difference in price between two similar options might be minimal, but if paying ten dollars more means your new jeans last twice as long as the other pair you were considering, then that is a win.

Take your purchasing power back from marketers, and choose a product that will prove a good investment of time, money, and resources.

BUY ETHICALLY

As well as quality in the product, consider what your purchase means for the quality of life of the people making it, and the impact

We need to let go of the idea of ownership as success and start to tap the resources that already exist.

on the environment. Ethical fashion and ethical manufacturing are blossoming subindustries, partly spurred by tragedies such as Bangladesh's Rana Plaza disaster in 2013, when more than 1,100 garment workers making clothes for many well-known mainstream brands perished in a factory collapse. While this event garnered a lot of attention simply because of the scale of the devastation, there are endless examples of similarly unsafe work conditions and unfair salaries for garment workers who bring us five-dollar T-shirts and jeans that cost less than a takeout pizza. What's even more offensive are the high-end labels charging massive amounts for clothes made in those same factories, where workers are paid the same paltry wages—as little as sixty dollars a month in some cases.

And while the human side of this story is the most tragic, the environmental pollution of fast fashion is second only to that of big oil companies. And this is only the fashion industry—we haven't even looked at construction, motor vehicles, electronics, furniture, palm oil...

We live in a time when we can make a difference and support brands that are being proactive on issues we care about. For me, those issues are fair working conditions for employees and sustainable manufacturing, which is why I support ethical brands like Patagonia. Whatever issues are most important to you, make a choice to support those doing good in the world, and acknowledge that you also have the ability to contribute to causes that are important to you simply by purchasing with intention.

○ ○ ○

To extricate ourselves from the ever-revolving cycle of want-buy-declutter-want-buy-reclutter, we need to figure out what's worth caring more about and what's worth caring less about. Moreover, think about how much relief you'll experience if you just care less about *stuff*. Once trends and forecasts and cutting-edge blah-blah mean less, you'll be able to unearth a new layer of contentment. It's been covered up by must-haves and this season's hottest new widgets, but it's there, waiting to help you forget all about the trends and comparisons, waiting to help you let go.

So care less. Start questioning those trends and whether your need is a true need or simply a want. Care less about your ego. Care less about ownership. Care less about fads. Care less about the opinions of people you will never know. And yes, care less about the Joneses.

But conversely, also care more. Care more about community and sharing resources. Care more about quality. Care more about the things you already own and use. Care more about the people making your stuff. Care more about the planet. If you do need to buy things, buy once, and buy well. Look for the best quality you can afford. Look for things

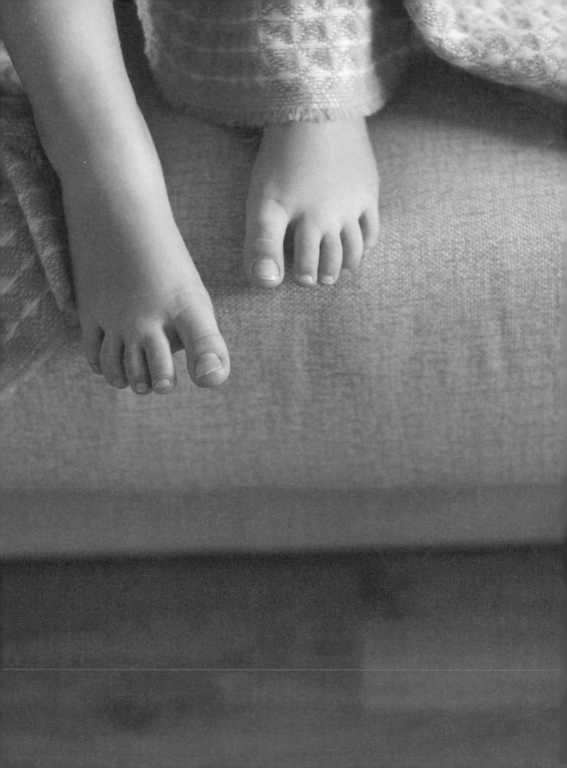

with multiple and varied uses. Look for items that can be passed on to someone else once you're finished with them. If you can afford to, buy the better-quality jeans, the sturdier lounge, the stroller that converts all the way up to a preschooler, the timeless sunglasses, the reusable coffee cups. Make it count, and make it worth the price you pay.

Even as I write these words, I feel a shadow of helplessness creeping over me: What do my actions matter? It can feel like you're a drop in the ocean—no one will notice, and nothing will change. Except that people *do* notice, and things *do* change. Over time, people start paying attention to what you're doing, how you're living, the choices you're making, and why you're making them. You stop spending your dollars, and a brand notices. You tell them why, and they hear you. You might feel inept in the face of it all, but your choices matter. And if enough of us join forces and start talking the same talk, people can't help but listen. And like the oft-quoted idea that as one person, we may not be able to change the world but may change the world for one person, we need to feel optimistic and confident that our choices do matter. So don't feel overwhelmed. Just start. Much like simplifying and decluttering, making consistent, small changes is going to propel you further ahead over time than taking one gigantic leap occasionally.

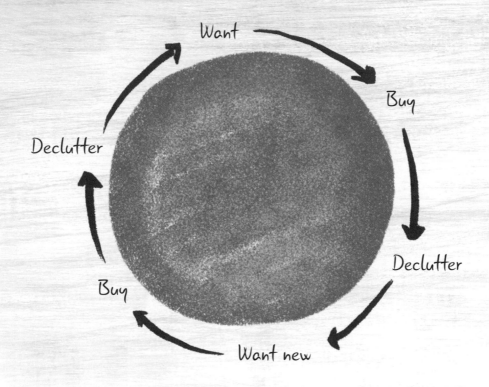

four

MINDFULNESS

Mindfulness. Everyone's tossing this buzz-word around, lauding it as an incredible cure-all for stress and busyness, ill health and procrastination. We have apps and conferences, special coloring books, retreats, and constant reminders popping up on social media of just how mindfully others are living. (Which begs the question: If a woman meditated on the beach but didn't take a selfie, did it really happen?)

For years, mindfulness was a Big Idea I wasn't nearly smart or evolved enough to understand, so I put it in the basket of woo that also held transcendental meditation, tarot reading, and crystal bathing. It intimidated me; therefore it wasn't valid.

The more I explored simplifying, though, the more I heard people espousing the benefits of living mindfully. But what did that *mean*? How could one live mindfully? What did it look like to live mindfully? To be a mindful person? I had no idea.

What I did understand, however, was mind-*less* living. And while I may not have been smart enough or enlightened enough to live mind-*fully*, mindlessness and I were on a first-name basis. In fact, we'd been intimate for a long time.

Every morning, I'd wake up and hit my snooze button a minimum of four times before I'd eventually roll over, pick up my phone, and mindlessly flick through my varied social media feeds and email inboxes for at least ten minutes longer than I had time for.

I would finally drag myself out of bed and eat breakfast hunched over my screen, not paying attention to the food I was eating or how it was making me feel. My family would wake up and join me as I shuffled things around in the kitchen and started to think about what I had on for the day. My phone would be nearby, and I'd turn it on every few minutes, checking in (with who or what, I couldn't tell you, but it made me feel important). Meanwhile, my kids would become less ready throughout the morning, and I'd become more stressed as I tried to do two hours' worth of tasks in the forty-five minutes I'd left myself.

I'd grind through the work of keeping things running at home, never being fully present in anything, whether that was playing, making a phone call, sending an email, or doing the laundry. My mind was always elsewhere, on the next thing I needed to do or somewhere I'd rather be. I was never completely where I actually was.

I'd mindlessly wish for the kids' nap time, when I'd mindlessly inhale lunch, again hunched over my screen, and again not actually registering the fact that I was eating. Then I'd race through the house while the kids slept, trying to get my to-do list under control. If they woke early or didn't sleep at all, the barely contained panic and frustration would bubble over, and I'd lose my temper. In fact, there used to be a large, star-shaped stain on our living room wall where I'd thrown a peach in utter frustration after one of our kids refused to sleep one hot summer afternoon.

I'd mindlessly snack my way through the afternoon, eating crappy food and drinking coffee, before dragging my tired, lethargic self through the dinner, bath, and bedtime routine, wishing the hours away. I'd push through the bedtime stories and endless good nights and collapse on the lounge where I'd mindlessly drink half a bottle of wine (at least) and flick through endless channels full of terrible TV before scrolling through my phone's various channels (Instagram, Facebook,

Twitter, email, news sites—at least twice each) before finally deciding to go to bed where I'd mindlessly scan my phone again, in case things had changed in the six minutes since I'd last looked, sleep fitfully, and wake to do it all again.

It sounds like a waking nightmare. And many days, it was. I was trapped and numb and completely disengaged from the people and the experiences around me.

I was an awful combination of depressed, anxious, overwhelmed, and completely lacking in self-confidence—and rather than face up to that, I'd built myself a thick armor that allowed me to barrel through my days. But the armor I'd built to protect me actually stopped me from feeling anything at all. And those days I barreled through? I can't remember them. I can't remember my daughter's hands on my face. I can't remember my baby son's cries. I can't remember feeling much love or kindness or joy. I mindlessly pushed through every block of twenty-four hours in order to get to the other side and do it again.

There is no joy in recounting this. It was brutal then, and it's brutal to revisit it now. But I share it with you because if I can come from a place of complete and utter mindlessness and begin to notice things, to wake up, to live mindfully, so can you.

When we first moved into our home in the mountains, we planted a garden in the backyard. What had previously been a typical suburban stretch of grass, paving, and a clothesline was given an upgrade as we planted lots of native grasses, shrubs, and plants, including a beautiful native climber called a hardenbergia, which we trained to grow up our timber fence. It was such a beautiful plant, with glossy green leaves dressed with delicate sprays of white and mauve flowers in early spring.

I loved planting and caring for that garden, feeling the dirt under my nails and the sun on my back, and I used to stare at it from my jewelry studio in the garage. But after our son was born, life spiraled out of control. The jewelry label closed, the garden was virtually abandoned, and I shuttered myself in the house for days at a time, only leaving to hang laundry on the clothesline or check the mail.

I'd spent a hot, busy summer decluttering our home and a long, grim winter trying to find tiny pockets of time for deep breathing and slowing my racing brain. One late winter morning, I walked past our neglected garden, and I noticed the first unfurling of flower sprays hanging from the hardenbergia, the slightest hint of an early blossom. It had changed overnight, I was sure of it, and was preparing to burst into flower.

Every morning, I'd walk out to hang the laundry and stop at the fence to inspect my flowers. I'd notice the change from the day before— the white tips of the buds growing larger and whiter each day, inching toward bloom. Then I began to notice other things—spiderwebs and ants and the tiny insects that called my garden home. I noticed the shadows and the way the sun made the leaves shine.

That winter had been long, stretching out for years of confusion,

sadness, anger, and exhaustion, but as those blossoms began to grow, something inside me woke up.

The morning I went to my garden and saw the first tiny, delicate flower where a day earlier there had been none was stunning. It was only a flower, but it was a flower where yesterday there had only been a bud. The changes that had to happen, the events that needed to occur for that single flower to come into being—it may have only been a tiny bloom, but it was an enormous miracle. I'd uncovered one of life's secrets, and I'd witnessed a miracle, all because I paid attention.

It sounds ridiculous, that this tiny change in the garden was so significant to me, but it's undeniable that from this first act of noticing came a slow trickle of more noticing.

At first, I spent time noticing things in solitude:

Dust motes drifting through the sun in our living room.

Fairy wrens returning to the jacaranda tree in our backyard.

The smell of jasmine in the air.

Slowly, that trickle of noticings became a stream that began to seep between the plates of my armor.

I noticed my daughter's eyes and the way they lit up whenever I said yes to playing.

I noticed the warm breath of my son as he slept on my chest.

I noticed the way my husband always kissed me goodbye in the mornings.

I noticed my heartbeat.

I noticed words and how they made me feel.

This stream gradually became a river of noticing—smiles and kindnesses, sunsets and opportunities, big things and small—and with it, mindfulness quietly arrived. I didn't realize it at the time, but this awareness, this tapping into the tiny details of life, was strong enough to gradually lift the plates of my armor and eventually wash them clean off.

As my raw, real, feeling self was revealed, two things began to happen. I began to experience more. More joy, yes, but also more realization, more discomfort, more pain, more bittersweetness. More awareness of the beauty and tragedy of life. For the first time in many years (maybe ever), I was becoming emotionally available, and it was stunningly uncomfortable.

The second thing that happened was I began engaging. I began really listening to what people were saying, considering what I was saying, and paying attention to what I was doing. I suddenly wanted more from life.

At this stage, our kids were four and two and full of an energy and joy I had never known. I was exhausted more often than not, as Ben was working long hours in the city, usually leaving before the kids woke and coming home after they'd gone to sleep. But I was alive and aware and had started doing things like dancing in the kitchen, laughing loudly, and rolling the car windows down, my favorite song turned up. I felt happy sometimes for no discernible reason (what is this sorcery?) and had begun writing again.

I don't know if kids of four and two have hobbies, but if they do, my kids would have nominated hide-and-seek as theirs. Every day, they played together, asking me to join them. Sometimes I'd play halfheartedly for five minutes, but usually, I'd say no. Or, more specifically, I'd tell them I would play once I'd finished folding the laundry, sending an email, or mopping the floor. I told them this because I knew they'd get distracted and forget five minutes later, so I wouldn't have to play.

One day, I was in the laundry when my daughter asked if I would play hide-and-seek with them. I told her no because I had too many things to do. Maybe later. She was used to me saying no (which, in regard to candy, is great, but in regard to spending time with her is sad) and simply walked away.

I don't know if it was the noticing or the waking up, the newly discovered voice of self-awareness or the look on her beautiful, open face, but the privilege of my position and the tragedy of my response hit me square in the chest. This sweet, rambunctious girl wanted to play with me. To her, I was special and important enough to invite into her arena of play, time and time again. Me. Imperfect, awkward me. And time and time again, I'd rebuff her, too busy with important grown-up things like laundry folding and floor mopping. I could have spent the next thirty minutes berating myself for being such a terrible parent, but instead, I went and found my kids, who by that stage had moved on to a particularly shrill game they called dinos and dollies, and I asked *them* if they wanted to play hide-and-seek. With me.

I will never forget the looks on their faces. It was joy and surprise and delight, and it woke something else in me. We played hide-and-seek all afternoon, and the thing I remember most is the tingly, giggly sense of excitement I had while hiding behind doors and under beds and in cupboards. It was a giddiness I hadn't felt since I was a kid, and it was a gift freely given from my own children that I could never repay. They'd helped me wake myself up to joy and wonder and playfulness.

Noticing began to have other impacts too. My previously barely contained temper was no longer explosive, and while I'm certain that leveling off had a lot to do with the antidepressants I was taking, once I came off those, my outbursts never returned. I was smiling more, and my confidence was slowly emerging. I was present in my daily life in a way I had never been before, and what's more, I believed I deserved to be.

As my garden bloomed and I spent a few beautiful moments every day noticing what was happening right in front of me, my battered emotional state was slowly improving, and we continued to simplify our home. Every carload of stuff that went to the secondhand shop was a fresh liberation, and I could feel that physical lightening in my shoulders. People had begun to comment that I looked happier, and I realized that for the first time, I had some buffer in my life, and it was insulating me from the brutal mood swings and brain snaps I'd experienced for years. Things were shifting.

Every day, I would find time to notice things, to practice tiny moments of mindfulness—spending time outside, breathing in the scent of flowers, studying the bees, and feeling the sun on my skin.

Other times, I would do thirty seconds of deep, slow breathing (in deep for the count of four, hold for four, out for four). I would complete these brief exercises and notice that the little pockets of peace had an immediate impact. If I was feeling overwhelmed or stressed, angry, or tired of being constantly touched and climbed on and demanded of, these small moments of mindfulness caused me to stop and gave me the opportunity to come out the other side and examine the problem with a more dispassionate eye. They gave me space.

But I wondered if these mindfulness practices were having a long-term impact. Was it really making a difference? Was I doing it right? Was I doing it wrong?

Much like decluttering, the big results weren't immediate. Sure, I'd feel a lightening of spirit or a sense of release if I sat and practiced deep breathing for five minutes, but I wasn't floating around in a Zen-like state of bliss, smiling peacefully at all who crossed my path. I still had bad days. I still struggled to be patient. I still got overwhelmed and frustrated.

I'm not a certified meditation practitioner, and I definitely don't have the qualifications to speak about the neurological benefits of mindfulness, but what I am qualified to share with you is this.

In the worst days of my depression and anxiety, I would snap regularly. There was a constant, low-grade whining in my head, and over time, it would ramp up. Every unexpected guest, every burnt dinner, every missed nap time—that whining grew louder until it was a shrieking panic inside my brain. Then something minor would happen—an innocuous comment or Ben getting home late from work—and I would simply snap. I'd cry and rage and convince myself that an adult tantrum was OK in this instance, because everything was just so bloody hard.

I had no margin. No room for change or flux. Mentally, I was operating beyond capacity, and when something happened that threw me, even a little, I had no room to expand. There was no buffer to help me cope, so I blew up.

There is no doubt that mindfulness helped me create that buffer. And when I recently looked back and realized I hadn't had a brain snap for years, it was both a shock and a relief. Living like that was exhausting.

My friend Bele talks about the mind being a sponge, made up of myriad tiny holes and gaps that fill up throughout the day. Work, friends, family, health, politics, news headlines, and social media updates fill these holes until the sponge is soaked through. And a soaking wet sponge is completely useless at mopping up spills, because it's already too full. What mindfulness does is give that sponge a gentle squeeze, releasing some of the excess and making space again, making the sponge effective once more.

And while I still don't float through my days in a blissful state, smiling in the face of frustration or joyfully reveling in the opportunity to swallow my pride, I operate at an even keel most days, and even during the most frazzled or hectic of times, I benefit constantly from the healthy amount of buffer I've created.

How to Practice Mindfulness

We humans tend to overcomplicate things. Mindfulness has morphed into Big Business. We pay a lot of money for people to teach us how to be mindful. We buy the apps, plug them into our smart watches, monitor outputs, and look at ways of optimizing our practices in order to spend the minimum time possible on eking out the maximum benefit. We've industrialized mindfulness, and now we believe it needs to be a Big Thing that we spend either time or money on every day. Preferably both.

But you can't outsource mindfulness. The right combination of app and course and book won't deliver a mindful life to your door by close of business the next day. No one can live mindfully for you. And while there are absolutely techniques and strategies that experts can teach, those techniques and strategies are useless unless they're implemented. Mindfulness is something you need to practice—yourself.

The wonderful news is you don't need five extra minutes a day. Not even one minute. Living a mindful life costs no money and will take no extra time. There is a payment involved, but I think you're good for it, because in order to live a mindful life you simply need to *pay attention*.

It is as simple and as difficult as that. Living mindfully is paying attention. It's noticing things. Tiny things. Enormous things. Miraculous things and things that make you smile. It's paying attention to what you feel, what you hear, taste, smell, and see. It's tapping into the emotions and responses you have. And you can do that literally wherever you find yourself, at any given moment in your day.

Standing in the kitchen, making a coffee? Pay attention to what you can hear, smell, taste. As you make your coffee, pay attention to your breath as it passes in and out of your nose. Feel the sensation of your feet on the floor and the sound of the hot water as it fills your cup.

Waiting in line at the grocery store? Get your head out of your phone and pay attention. How are your shoulders? Slumped? Straighten them up. How does that make you feel? What about the people around you? What are they doing? Are they chatting? Are they ignoring each other? Smiling, making eye contact? How about the person who serves you at the register? Did you say hello? What was his response? Was he surprised or bored or both?

Commuting on the train? Put on a beautiful piece of music and sit with your eyes closed, feeling the gentle rocking of the car as it moves you toward your work or your home. Listen, truly listen, to the music. The lyrics, the changes in tempo. What does it make you feel? What memories does it bring up?

None of these things has cost you anything except attention. It's simply a matter of choosing to notice. And that, dear reader, is mindfulness.

There are, of course, many other ways of bringing mindfulness into your day, but this simple act of noticing was my entry point, and it changed my perspective in enormous and tiny important ways.

If you don't know where to start, begin by noticing, wandering, exploring, and being filled with wonder. Once we start waking up, even the most mundane, everyday things can become miracles.

But mindfulness can also be a specific practice, something you enjoy doing simply for the escape it offers, for the sheer joy of it, for the sensations or the process.

Mindfulness can be the simple art of paying attention, but it is also:

- being creative
- getting outside
- growing something
- doing nothing
- practicing yoga
- moving your body

Notice your breath. Notice your body—the way it moves, the way it responds and reacts. The way it feels when you take care of it. The way it feels when you don't. Notice imperfection. Notice the things you're grateful for, and notice how many other things there are that deserve your gratitude. Notice nature. Notice how you feel when you get outside. Notice movement—in your body, your breath, the way your loved ones' fingers curl around yours, the way light dances across the ceiling, the way the breeze kisses your face. These things are all mindfulness.

- deep breathing
- taking stock of your senses
- silent walking
- noticing something you've never noticed before
- exercising
- enjoying something beautiful

- paying attention to the person you're with
- laughing
- absorbing the music
- spreading kindness
- smiling
- exploring meditation

BEING CREATIVE

Coloring or sketching, writing poetry or fiction, painting, sculpting, cooking, stitching, knitting, or crocheting can all be acts of mindfulness. The act, the process of creating, brings us to the present moment, allowing us to leave behind concerns of our past and worries for the future. Making, rather than consuming, is a beautiful act of mindfulness.

GETTING OUTSIDE

By taking a moment to connect with nature, we become part of something larger, and by learning to love and appreciate the natural world around us, we begin to treasure it. Living a sustainable, connected life begins in the outdoors. We won't fight for what we don't love, and getting to know nature is a surefire way to care for this planet we call home.

The simple act of sitting and taking in some sunshine, watching the clouds, or feeling the breeze also connects us to the moment and the seasons in a vital way. Try leaning against a tree (or hugging one!), going for a hike, eating lunch in the park with your shoes off and your feet on the grass, going for a walk in the rain and splashing in puddles, or paying attention to the birds or bees flying around.

GROWING SOMETHING

Gardening as mindfulness is wonderful, and you don't need a garden or even a balcony to experience it, just a pot in a sunny position, some seeds, a little water, and care. Paying attention to the way the seed slowly opens to create a sprout. Gently watering and caring for that sprout as it grows its first two leaves, watching those first leaves multiply, and noticing as the stem strengthens and grows upward. Seeing how the plant reacts to water, light, food. And if you grow something edible like herbs or tomatoes, it's about the most delicious form of mindfulness there is.

DOING NOTHING

Fight the urge to connect with your phone and simply be. Be still and listen to your thoughts, feel your feelings, and recognize the urge to break the nothingness with action. Learn to let that urge pass, and you're learning to acknowledge a desire without acting on it. You're learning that gratification doesn't need to be immediate and that often those cravings and urges will pass.

PRACTICING YOGA

There is a saying my yoga teacher repeats often: "Let go of the thoughts and feelings that no longer serve you." And while I believe negative thoughts and feelings often serve an important purpose, I also believe we hold on to them much longer than we need to. Learning how to be in the moment, in the bubble of my yoga practice, is a tremendously useful skill and one that has fueled so many other changes—physical, mental, and emotional. It's not just about the poses, but the expectation that we turn up fully every time we step on to the mat.

MOVING YOUR BODY

Activities such as stretching, dancing, rock climbing, walking, skiing, or surfing can all be beautiful forms of mindfulness, while also letting us move our bodies without stepping foot inside a gym. Tapping into what our bodies are doing and how they feel puts us right in the moment, making us completely present.

DEEP BREATHING

Take ten deep, slow breaths into your belly while thinking about the movement of the air through your nose, down your throat, into your

inhale for four

hold for four

exhale for four

hold for four

repeat

lungs, and back out again. Focus on the expansion of your belly and your lungs with each breath, and keep a slow, steady count. It's one of the simplest forms of mindfulness, and it is accessible to everyone, at any time.

Try taking an extra thirty seconds in the bathroom to take some deep breaths, or stay in the car for one minute and use that time to reconnect with your breath. There are pockets of time there for you, and the good news is they can be very brief but still have a positive impact.

TAKING STOCK OF YOUR SENSES

What can you see right now? Perhaps it's your computer or your living room. Look closer. What else can you see? Dust motes? Sunshine? A plant or trees outside the window? The reflection of lights in your monitor? What else?

What can you hear? People talking, the whirr of computer hard drives, your kids playing in the next room, your dog snoring? Maybe someone is mowing their lawn or printing documents. Can you hear your own breath? Your own heartbeat? Is it fast, or is it slow?

What can you feel? The seat under your butt? Is it hard or soft? The ground under your feet, perhaps the chill of air-conditioning, or the coffee still warming your mouth? Can you feel tension in your shoulders? What about your face? Is it tense or relaxed? Your jaw, is it clenched or soft?

What can you smell? Fresh air? Coffee? Perfume? Cleaning products?

What can you taste? Your tea? Perhaps your lunch still lingers? Search deeper—what about your lunch or your tea can you taste? Is it sweet or bitter, salty or sour?

By taking a few minutes to examine your senses, you bring yourself wholly into the present moment and put the pressures, stress, and worries of yesterday or tomorrow out of mind for just a moment. You're giving yourself the gift of a buffer.

SILENT WALKING

There is constant stimulus in modern life, and the opportunity to let thoughts out rather than cramming more in is a rare one. By walking in silence, with no music, no podcasts, no audiobooks, we invite our thoughts to do their thing without impediment. So often, I will have a breakthrough in these moments of silence, as my thoughts, which need time to roll around in silence and put themselves in some kind of order, gradually work themselves out.

A mindfulness moment. What can you see right now? What can you hear? What can you feel? What can you smell? What can you taste?

NOTICING SOMETHING YOU'VE NEVER NOTICED BEFORE

What is happening around you that you've never noticed before? This is an invitation to look a little deeper, pay a little more attention, remove the lens of sameness that the day in, day out routine places over our eyes. What can you see? The way the light hits your coffee table or the pattern on the carpet in your doctor's waiting room. The swirl of your fingerprints or the creases in a tree trunk. By switching to noticing mode, we immediately bring ourselves to the present. It can be as simple as that.

EXERCISING

Use your time at the gym as a form of mindfulness simply by focusing on how it makes you feel. Lifting weights, cycling, maintaining a plank, or enduring the burn of a squat are all telling you what is happening in your body, and to pay attention is to be right there, present and aware.

ENJOYING SOMETHING BEAUTIFUL

To examine a piece of art, read a poem, or listen to a beautiful piece of music is to focus closely upon it and wonder how was it made. It's to be curious about the methods and materials went into its creation, the level of craftsmanship and mastery the creator possesses, and what her motivation was in putting it out into the world. Art is anything designed to make you feel something, and spending time with those feelings is an amazing way to tap into a deeper moment.

PAYING ATTENTION TO THE PERSON YOU'RE WITH

Stop and notice the specific color of their eyes or the way their hand covers their mouth when they laugh, the exact tone of their voice, or the downy hair on the tops of their arms. Try putting your phone away and listening deeply to not only what they're saying, but how they're saying it. By doing these things, you're creating a deeper memory of this person for yourself and also being completely present with them.

LAUGHING

A big belly laugh is a catharsis, a therapy, a release. Find things that make you laugh, and spend time immersed in them. Podcasts, TV shows, live comedy, or books by funny people. Life doesn't need to be so serious. Get working on those laugh lines.

ABSORBING THE MUSIC

Good music can bring you to tears. Find what you love, and listen to it. Dance to it. Let it move you to sing or swing or cry or jive. Listen closely to it, and concentrate on what you hear—the lyrics, the changes

in tempo, the different instruments, and the way they each contribute to a whole that is greater than the sum of its parts.

SPREADING KINDNESS

Think about ways you can spread kindness from where you are—get a cup of tea for your partner, or send a text to friends just to let them know you love them. These might be small acts, but doing them regularly helps us to tap into the humanity that surrounds us and the fact that we can impact each other in big ways by doing a small thing with kindness.

SMILING

It's completely free to smile at someone. Do it with regularity, and don't let yourself be concerned with the response of the other person. Some will be surprised, some will be suspicious, some will respond with their own face-splitting grin, while others will scowl. That's OK.

EXPLORING MEDITATION

Explore different kinds of meditation—silent, guided, loving kindness, and sleep meditation, for example—and see which works for you. There are great apps and podcasts to guide you, as well as courses and classes. There is so much peace and self-reflection to be found in meditation, not to mention the benefits to our well-being, productivity, and overall mental health.

○ ○ ○

I could end this chapter here and feel like I'd done a pretty good job of expressing how simple it is to live a mindful life. But we humans really do enjoy complicating things, so I also want to look at the most common roadblocks we throw in our own way as we try to adopt mindfulness.

I HAVE NO TIME

You don't really need to give this any time. There are so many ways to adopt mindfulness in your current day that the argument of not enough time is completely moot. Choose one task you already do, and turn it into a mindfulness moment:

- hanging the laundry
- making a cup of tea
- driving to soccer practice
- warming your lunch in the office microwave

Simply pay attention to what you're doing in that moment—the sensations, actions, smells, and tastes. That's mindfulness.

I'M NOT GOOD AT IT

Great! No one is "good" at mindfulness. In fact, sometimes practicing mindfulness brings about more awareness, which can feel really uncomfortable. It can bring you back to consciousness, which often means seeing truths we're not always happy to see. Don't let that stop you, because only from awareness can we learn how to change and adapt.

If we remove the idea of good or bad from mindfulness (or meditation, or most things, really) and simply view it as a part of our efforts to create a slower, simpler life, we can also remove the stigma of not getting it right. View it as an experiment instead. Don't attach any particular outcomes to the practices of mindfulness; simply wait and see how you feel.

I'M NOT THAT KIND OF PERSON

I used to think the same thing about certain types of meditation and other practices (like chakra cleansing, for example, which I am now exploring with curiosity, playfulness, and, OK, a little skepticism). But what I was really saying is that I was afraid of it. I didn't know anything about it, and that scared me.

If you really don't want to meditate, then don't. Instead of diving straight into thirty-minute meditations or yoga classes, try adding a touch of mindfulness to things you already enjoy doing. Love gardening? Use that as a practice. Love guitar? Make that your time of mindfulness. Or simply start noticing more.

I'M SKEPTICAL ABOUT ITS USEFULNESS

It's easy to be skeptical of a slow fix when we're constantly bombarded with instant gratification, seven-day miracle cures, and easy solutions to help you lose thirty pounds in thirty-two seconds! There is no miracle cure, and there is no one-off fee that will create mindfulness for you. And while there are many studies showing the positive effects of mindfulness and meditation on our brains and our well-being, you're probably not going to believe it until you experience it yourself anyway.

Be playful and curious, and instead of attaching a predetermined result to it, simply experiment. Try some of the suggestions in this book for a week at a time, and see how you feel.

I DON'T KNOW HOW

First of all, join the club! Secondly, see above. There is really no how, only noticing.

I GET BORED

We're so used to constant stimulus that the absence of it immediately triggers boredom, or fear or anxiety or twitchiness. Instead of giving into that boredom, see it for what it is—your brain lashing out, looking for a fix. You don't need to sit there peacefully feeling bored, but you can sit there and acknowledge how you feel. Stick that boredom in the corner, and continue to sit, continue to notice, continue to be.

I CAN'T SIT STILL

Then don't. Go for a walking meditation. Use your gym workout as a mindfulness practice. Garden or paint or write or sew in mindfulness.

I CAN'T STOP MY THOUGHTS

You don't need to. Thinking is what our brains do, and rather than trying to stop our thoughts from zooming around, simply accept that they are doing what thoughts do. You can acknowledge their presence (give 'em a little wave if you want to) and continue your mindfulness practice, knowing that if they're important, these thoughts won't go far. Hint: often, they're not important.

I FEEL TOO MANY FEELINGS

We do a *lot* to avoid feelings like anxiety, sadness, or anger. We stay busy, we self-medicate, we say yes, we say no—all so as not to experience the "bad" feelings life has for us. But these feelings are important, because in order to feel the highs of joy and happiness, we also need to understand the lows of grief, envy, or disappointment. Mindfulness allows us to acknowledge and accept such feelings, feel them in all their depth, and understand that they are valid and important. It also helps us to understand that they are not everything—even on days that feel like sadness has swallowed the world.

Learning to distinguish your feelings from the truth is another huge benefit of ongoing mindfulness practices. We listen to the voices of negative self-talk, criticism, and nastiness, and it's so easy to believe them. But simply because our brains are telling us something doesn't make those thoughts true, and by pausing, questioning, and analyzing those negative ideas, we gain the ability to see and name our feelings without needing to immerse ourselves in them. Just because they're there doesn't mean we need to engage with them, and just because we think them doesn't mean those thoughts are true.

IT DOESN'T MAKE A DIFFERENCE

Some days, maybe it doesn't. But just like you can't judge the usefulness of French lessons by your fluency after day one, you can't judge the effectiveness of mindfulness practice after staring at a flower for two minutes. Focus on the moment it *is* impacting, and understand that you're giving yourself the gift of time, of buffer and space, regardless of how blissed out you do or don't feel.

o o o

In this day and age of Big, Fast Solutions (guaranteed six-pack in six minutes! Follow these three steps to make $300,000 by midnight!), we've become accustomed to the claim of big, fast results. But when it comes to living a mindful life, they don't exist.

And while that might challenge our thoroughly modern expectation of a one-hit, overnight cure-all, it's actually one of the biggest benefits to living a mindful life.

As a human, you will stumble, and you will backslide. I'm constantly doing both when things get busy or I tell myself I no longer need the mindfulness practices I've worked so hard to establish. Thankfully, mindfulness is an incredibly forgiving lifestyle, because there are so many accessible ways to practice, and it's easy to regroup and start again. Missed a few weeks of meditation? That's OK. Just add some single tasking or deep breathing to your day. Forgotten how it feels to wander an art gallery or take a hike in the woods? No problem. If you don't have time for that, why not take a minute to watch the clouds pass by instead?

Living mindfully and having an extensive tool kit of mindfulness exercises to draw from means you will be able to find the right tool for the job, regardless of how stressed, busy, or tired you are. And the more you expand your tool kit, the more ways you can adopt mindfulness into your everyday life without feeling like it's just another chore on a to-do list that's already too long.

Mindfulness will also teach you a great deal about yourself if you let it. Once you begin to get familiar with the resistance, the inner reasoning, the self-talk that accompanies your efforts, you'll start to gain some powerful insights into yourself that might otherwise have remained buried.

Since starting meditation, I have learned so much about my self-confidence and the bullshit stories I tell myself about myself, because they were the thoughts I was hearing (and believing) time and time again. Learning to observe them, give them a little wave of recognition, and then firmly ignore them has given me a freedom, lightness, and confidence I've never had before.

Being able to form positive habits, to have strong willpower and decision-making muscles is another by-product of mindfulness that has incredibly positive implications. Learning to establish positive habits in the ways we think and experience the world translates to an ability to form better habits around what we eat, how we move, and what actions we choose to take. Mindfulness, and specifically meditation, have helped me to completely transform my previously mindless eating and drinking habits, significantly reduce my procrastination levels, and pay close attention to the way my body feels both with and without regular exercise.

So while you may initially think that sitting and deep breathing for three minutes is doing very little other than using up three minutes, there are many other ways mindfulness will impact your life.

a mindfulness tool kit

five

DISCONNECT TO RECONNECT

Modern connection technology has delivered us a paradox. We have more connection and less humanity. We're hyper-engaged and increasingly isolated. We have more information and less critical thought. We see more tragedy and have less empathy. We enjoy more privilege but are less satisfied. We are sensitive to personal offense and desensitized to the suffering of others.

The connected world offers us so much—so much to learn, to see, to share, to do. But hyperconnection brings with it a steep downside.

Slow living provides an opportunity to step back, pay attention, and question the ways we use technology, to recalibrate our relationship with the constantly switched-on, logged-in world. It offers us an opportunity to disconnect in order to reconnect.

It occurred to me recently as I read Stephen King's book *The Stand* that most of the books I read are postapocalyptic fiction, worlds where much of our modern technology no longer exists.

The Walking Dead, the Wool trilogy, *The Stand*, Margaret Atwood's MaddAddam trilogy, Emily St. John Mandel's *Station Eleven*—no phones, no internet, no social media. No notifications trilling at 3:00 a.m., no emails requiring an immediate response. Of course, there's also no banking, no communication, no news services, no travel, no medical records. Modern society clings on as a shell of its former self, at best.

I'm no Luddite; I own a smartphone and a laptop that I use every day. I love the internet. I wouldn't have the job I do without it. There are so many benefits to our connected world, and I'm not here to suggest we should get rid of them.

So why do I find the idea of these post-smartphone, post-Twitter, postapocalyptic worlds so appealing?

Peace.

That peacefulness *would* be severely compromised by the existence of zombies, but ignoring that particular complication for a moment, I think it's the idea of not being constantly available, or the expectation that I will be, that I find most attractive.

We've reached peak information, peak connectedness, and peak availability, and I know I'm not alone in feeling overwhelmed by it. The good news is we can create that peace for ourselves without unleashing Captain Trips or some other kind of super flu on the world, and we don't need to give up the incredible benefits of modern, connected technology in order to do it.

Let me say this first: technology has delivered us the gift of connection and, with it, so many other wonderful benefits.

COMMUNITY

We can connect and find a tribe of like-minded people. We can add our voices to a movement and share stories with others. We can read a blog or listen to a podcast and realize we're not alone in our thoughts/struggles/sadness/passions.

COMMUNICATION

We can get in touch with friends or family immediately, across massive distances. We can reach out to people we admire, people who inspire us, people who have helped us. We can communicate a message or a worldview easily. We can talk to colleagues and peers remotely, and we can send a letter to another country and receive a response in under a minute, where the same communication used to take months.

EDUCATION

We can learn from experts and study almost any topic over great distances. We can research and go deep on a subject we're fascinated by, and we have access to books, lectures, courses, and learning institutions so we can devote ourselves to it.

SELF-IMPROVEMENT

We can use technology for motivation and inspiration. We can use it to learn how to meditate, improve our running style, or practice yoga in our living rooms. We can learn how to cook or speak another language. We can be mentored and join accountability groups. We can tap into the experiences of strangers and learn from the changes they've made, and we can use their achievements to drive ourselves to betterment.

AWARENESS

Technology enables us to learn more about world events, see beyond the bubble of our own country, our own town, our own friends. It exposes us to stories we may never have known about and brings down fences we might never have known existed.

OPPORTUNITY

We can work remotely. We can work flexibly. We can answer emails from home. Take a call out of hours. Make a video call. There are jobs that wouldn't exist without the internet and the opportunities that technology has created. We can build a platform, share our words, our videos, our photos. We can launch businesses and collaborate.

EXPOSURE

Now we discover ideas, music, films, books, writers, creators we may not have known otherwise. Our lives can become enriched by engaging with people outside our direct circles. Our world can get bigger and smaller at the same time.

o o o

We choose to place value on hyperconnection. We choose to value likes and hearts and follows. And sometimes we choose to value those things over depth or truth or authenticity (as opposed to #authenticity).

We choose to use social media to tell stories about ourselves, to signal the kind of person we want the world to think we are. We choose to tie our self-esteem to those stories, and we choose to find inspiration in a social media profile rather than our friends, family, job, passion, planet.

The technology isn't the problem; it's how we choose to use it. And it is a choice.

We choose to keep our phones in our pockets.

We choose to put them on the dinner table.

We choose to respond to emails at 11:00 p.m.

We choose to update statuses when we're sick, or in bed, or on vacation, or while someone who loves us waits for us to look at them.

We choose to document an endless succession of precious, personal moments, and we choose to view so much of our life through a screen.

What are we missing out on while our faces are glued to our screens? What experiences have been crowded out? What do we have less of? What do we no longer have or know or do or feel because we're so constantly connected?

TIME

We get online to check our email and, seventeen minutes later, have watched three funny videos, looked at our bank balance, retweeted something, scanned each of our social media channels, and not actually responded to any emails.

On any given day, I could waste an hour or more by giving in to digital distraction. A cat video here, a viral tweet there, weather checking, Facebook scrolling, news surfing. None of it actually achieving anything other than a mindless consumption of information I didn't need. We may complain we don't have enough time to do all the things we want to do, but how true can that be when we find enough time to waste an hour?

EMPATHY

We've become adept at creating separation between the online person and the real-life person. We don't see the human behind the profile picture. We unintentionally view tragedy, war, and violence through a lens of entertainment. We see trolling, bullying, and negative comments

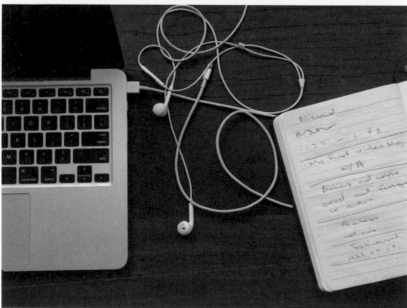

every time we get online, and it becomes the norm to see people treat each other with disdain, even outright hatred. Over time, we simply get used to it—until it happens to us.

DIVERSITY

Conversely, we've decided that any opinion that is different from ours, any criticism, any worldview, is the work of a troll or a hater. So we shut it down. We ridicule those who just don't get it. And we end up with our own echo chamber full of people who think like us, people who won't challenge our opinions, people who tell us we're right because they're right.

ACTION

Clicking "like" on a post about refugees or sharing a video about an environmental issue that's important to you is a great way to create awareness for a cause you're passionate about. The more people who know about it, the better, right? But we so often stop there. And while awareness is important, charities don't run on awareness, starving people can't eat awareness, and awareness alone won't change the world. Clicking a button or changing our profile picture simply makes us feel comfortable, like we're doing something while scrolling through our phones.

MEANING

It's so easy to misread intention or tone on a computer monitor or phone screen, and an innocuous comment can become an insult without ever intending to offend. And because we don't see any nonverbal cues when reading an email or a text message, we often find ourselves wondering what they meant by that comment. Consider the mental energy we expend every time we worry about the true meaning of the text or the emoji. (What does the unicorn emoticon mean in that context anyway? Am I the unicorn? Is she? Is that a joke? Or a gibe?)

DISCERNMENT

Instead of scrolling past the comments section we know will infuriate us, we look anyway and then…wind up infuriated. There is a difference between being open to other worldviews and diving headfirst into a comment section of rage, hatred, and vitriol. We don't need to engage in the drama, and yet we're drawn to it, rubbernecking as we go past the car crash.

DOWNTIME

We constantly feel "on." We feel pressured to respond to messages immediately or worry that our friends, family, clients will be upset. Weekends and evenings are no longer downtime. Holidays and vacation aren't either. And the dilemma is that the quicker we respond, the more likely the sender will expect a faster response next time.

CONFIDENCE

The endless comparisons of social media are exhausting and damaging. We either compare ourselves to others and feel less than them (our vacations aren't as amazing, our desk isn't as tidy, our yoga isn't as impressive, our kids aren't as well dressed, our bookshelf isn't as color coordinated), or we compare ourselves to others and feel superior (our vacation is better, our desk is styled, our yoga is bendy, our kids are immaculate, our bookshelves are Instagram worthy). In either case, this is a game we will never win, and as long as we keep playing it, we'll never find contentment.

FOCUS

We use the internet to distract us when we should be working, studying, paying bills, cleaning, talking to people, or playing with our kids. We use it to avoid discomfort or work or people or responsibilities or deadlines. We use it to convince ourselves we're busy. We're using technology as a diversion, rather than the useful tool it should be.

o o o

If we can apply only one idea to
technology as we move forward, it needs
to be mindfulness. We need to make our
use of technology intentional. Use it well.
Use it to make life better. And then put
it down and go do something else.

Slow living is a call to disconnect. Switch off our phones and get outside. Talk to people at the coffee shop. Offer a stranger an anonymous kindness. Volunteer our time to others. Have a spirited conversation with someone who doesn't see the world like we do. Invite depth to our lives. Feel the sun on our faces. View the night sky. Sit around a campfire. Listen to an entire album. Turn off the GPS and see what you discover. Use a phrasebook in a foreign country. Smile at someone with our face, not our keyboard. Give our time or our money to causes that need it. Stand up and stand for something. Have a voice. Protest or support. Pay attention to the person sitting next to us. Pay attention to the child whose eyes so often only see yours turned away.

How do we do this, though? When connection is so ingrained, how do we learn to embrace disconnection?

Start small, start slow, and start with awareness.

There are times when you do need to be connected. Perhaps you're on call, or maybe you work in customer service and it's your job to respond to messages in a timely manner. Maybe an elderly relative has you on speed dial, or you've left the kids with a babysitter. Fine.

But just like we can use other people's clutter as an excuse for not dealing with our own ("Why bother? It won't make a big difference anyway."), don't let this become your excuse for being constantly connected.

Ask yourself:

- Is this making life better? In a real way?
- Am I learning something? Is it worthwhile?
- Am I avoiding something? What is it?
- If this is causing comparisons, negativity, or anger, why am I still here?
- If it's bringing positive feelings of validation, popularity, or connection, can I find that elsewhere?
- Should I be sleeping?
- Should I be working?
- Are there people here who want to spend time with me?

When our kids were really young, I saw a public service announcement that showed a scene through the eyes of an adult and the same scene through the eyes of his child. The pair sat at the dining table, side by side. The father was on his phone, doing something very adult-important. Reading emails, maybe. And as far as the dad was concerned, he was spending time with his kid. They were together. They were having quality time. He was happy with his efforts to do two things at once.

The kid, however, couldn't see his dad at all, because a wall had been put up between them.

I've never forgotten it. That we can so easily convince ourselves we're completely present when we're, at best, distracted and, at worst, totally absent in all ways but the physical. It's one of the reasons we've established some simple boundaries in our home to keep technology where it belongs—in the toolbox, not attached to our bodies.

NO SCREENS AT THE TABLE

This is a simple rule that everyone in our house understands and occasionally ignores. But the fact that it's repeated like a mantra means everyone is aware of it and will call others out if we "forget."

Eating dinner together is one of my favorite times of the day (even when the conversation revolves around how much the kids don't want to eat the food one of us has cooked). We talk to each other. We ask about one another's days, and we ask the same questions every night: "What was a good part of your day today?" and "What was a not-so-good part of your day?"

The answers are often enlightening, helping us get to know each other more and giving the kids a chance to share part of their day on their own terms. I know if we were to eat in front of the TV or if I had my phone out, these conversations just wouldn't happen.

Slow living is about quality time and making things count. These conversations matter. We listen to each other. We annoy each other, sure, but we love each other immensely, and we turn up.

TECHNOLOGY BOUNDARIES:

No screens at the table

Screen-free bedrooms

No screens in the morning

Minimal technology during the week

Remove notifications

Remove visual reminders

Take regular breaks

Create a pre-bed, post-wake-up ritual

Only check social media on one device

Only check emails when you have time

to answer them

Leave your phone behind

Set time limits

Take a digital sabbatical

Go off the grid

Remove apps from the phone

SCREEN-FREE BEDROOMS

Ben and I have never had a TV in the bedroom, because I knew it would impact our sleep, but somehow I'd never considered that our phones or iPads would have the same (if not greater) effect on our ability to get good rest. I would read books on my iPad every night and wake up to my phone alarm each morning. I'd then roll over and scroll through emails, social media, and news updates before I got out of bed, and the weight of that information would settle on my shoulders before the day had even begun.

Mind you, I never did anything with the emails or the social media; I didn't actually answer them. They just sat there, in my brain, for hours before I took any kind of action.

When Ben and I completed a sleep experiment that called for no screens in the bedroom for a month, I was amazed by how much faster I fell asleep, how much better quality that sleep was, how much more time I had in the mornings, and how much more energy I had throughout the day. It turns out that it wasn't just the amount of sleep that was having an impact, but also the quality of that sleep. And the blue light of modern screens not only mimics daylight, telling our brains it's time to get up and work, but it also affects our ability to get into the deeper REM sleep cycle, meaning that even if we did get to sleep after being on a screen in the evening, we never got deep, restorative sleep, and we woke up tired every day.

Staying off screens for an hour before bed and not waking to my phone in the morning has cut down on my technology use massively, and I now get up, practice yoga, meditate, shower, get dressed, and make a cup of tea before I've looked at any screens at all. I can greet the morning well rested and know I've already practiced self-care in the time it used to take me to roll out of bed and think about the day ahead.

Additionally, there is now no temptation to wake up in the middle of the night and check my phone. This used to happen more than I'd like to admit (probably because I wasn't sleeping deeply, after scrolling through my phone before turning off the lights), and often I wouldn't get back to sleep after that "quick" check.

NO SCREENS IN THE MORNINGS

Similarly, Ben and I now *try* to keep the mornings, until 9:00 a.m.-ish, a screen-free zone. It doesn't always happen—I'll go and write if I'm up early enough, and Ben will often get a start on work before the kids have gone to school, but we're very mindful of it.

MINIMAL TECHNOLOGY DURING THE WEEK

This applies to the kids mostly, who both own iPads but aren't allowed to use them from Sunday through Friday afternoon. They also aren't allowed to play video games during the week, and the only tech they have access to is the computer for homework purposes and TV on an occasional rainy afternoon. The gadgets live on top of the fridge, and we use the afternoons to do things like swimming, reading, gardening, playing outside, or going for a short hike.

○ ○ ○

Boundaries are great for drawing a line in the sand and saying, "No more." But how do we better manage our use of technology when we need to use it? How can we avoid procrastination and meaningless scrolling?

These strategies aren't always going to apply, but what each of them has done so well for me over the past few years is to make me more aware of how often I'm using technology, how it's making me feel, and how frequently I use it to distract me from something more important. They also help break the habit of constantly checking in, rewiring my brain to not automatically open Facebook or quickly check my emails every time I open my phone.

They're all really simple ideas, and many, rather ironically, use technology.

The only problem is that they seem so simple, so insignificant, so easy to do, that surely they can't be useful. So if you're anything like me, you'll ignore them. But then I remember I turned my life around completely by decluttering my handbag, so I figure it's not too much of a stretch to think we can create peace in our days by adopting some of these super simple ideas too.

REMOVE NOTIFICATIONS

There is nothing more distracting than a constantly buzzing device, and research now shows it can take up to twenty-three minutes to return to our original task once we've been distracted by a beeping phone or an incoming email.

By removing all notifications from your phone and only checking in a handful of times (preferably at the same time each day), you resist the temptation of "just checking to see who that was," which invariably leads to further distraction and loss of concentration.

REMOVE VISUAL REMINDERS

Similarly, by removing visual cues of unopened emails or unattended social media notifications, we take away the endorphin rush of the little red circle that's telling us we're wanted, we've been noticed, or someone likes or needs us.

- Put your phone in a drawer if you're working on other tasks.
- Close the email account on your computer and only check in every hour or two.

- Move all your social media apps to the final screen on your smartphone so you don't immediately see the unread notifications if you happen to look at your phone for something else.

TAKE REGULAR BREAKS

Nominate some off-line time every day. Even if it's taking a walk around the block without your phone or setting aside two hours each day for phone-in-drawer time, taking a regular break from your screens helps build a buffer into your days.

Similarly, try to find a twenty-four-hour period every week (we try for lunchtime Saturday to lunchtime Sunday) where you disconnect from all social media, email, and phone use.

CREATE A PRE-BED, POST-WAKE-UP RITUAL

Aim to have the last hour of your night and the first hour of your day as designated screen-free times. Set an alarm for one hour before your usual bedtime, and use this as a reminder to turn off all screens.

Similarly, try staying off your phone and computer until after you've dressed and had breakfast.

The evening break makes it easier for you to do some reading, take a bath, or have a chat with a loved one, while also helping you to have more and better quality sleep. And the tech-free morning allows a

gentle, productive start to the day, with minimal wasted time and no email hangover to contend with as you get ready for the day.

ONLY CHECK SOCIAL MEDIA ON ONE DEVICE

By nominating only one device on which you can check and interact on social media, you cut down on the ways in which you can distract yourself. If you choose to only check Facebook and Twitter on your computer, you immediately gain back the time you'd normally spend scrolling through them on your smartphone, and you need to physically sit at your desk in order to do so. Making it that little bit less convenient is a great way of slowly breaking a mindless habit and has seen me cut way down on my incidental scrolling time.

ONLY CHECK EMAILS WHEN YOU HAVE TIME TO ANSWER THEM

This is a simple change to make but one that has taught me the power of intention. I would often check my emails, hoping there was something in my inbox that made me feel needed and important, but would rarely respond to those emails at the same time.

The ego boost of the email was the fix I was looking for, rather than the communication itself, and once I understood my reasons for the constant checking in, I could make the changes necessary to stop wasting my time and start getting productive. So now I try to only check

my emails when I have the time or the capacity to answer them. It's a simple change that has made a huge difference to the state of my inbox, as well as my email return rate.

LEAVE YOUR PHONE BEHIND

I don't love the generational comparisons of, "Well, back in my day..." But when I was a kid, no one had a mobile phone, and if you went out somewhere, you were pretty much uncontactable. You'd make plans to meet someone at a later time, and you'd tell them where you were going if they needed to get in touch. At the risk of sounding old, I really miss that.

If you're popping down to the store, it's OK to leave your phone behind. Going out for a coffee or out to dinner, heading off on a run or to visit a friend, it's OK to not always be on call.

Ben and I will often leave our phones at home if we go out for a coffee, and I'm still amazed at just how naked I feel without it. It's a good kind of vulnerability, as it removes another layer of disconnect and leaves us with conversations and people watching, as opposed to status updates and text notifications, but it's always humbling to realize just how normal we feel when we're constantly connected.

SET TIME LIMITS

Put Parkinson's law to the test (where a task will expand to fill the time it's given) and give yourself a time limit for social media each day. There are numerous apps and plugins that allow you to nominate an amount of time (thirty minutes a day is a good place to start) in which you're allowed on to particular websites.

Similarly, giving yourself a time limit (I like aiming for an hour) in which to answer your emails each day is another way of compressing a task to a handful of very intentional blocks of time. By giving myself thirty minutes in the middle of the day and thirty minutes at the end of the day in which to answer all the emails requiring a response, I find my answers are more to the point and more likely to be sent in a timely manner. Whereas if email becomes an open-ended task, it gradually begins to swallow my entire day, and I overwrite and overthink my responses.

o o o

The gadgets we use have been designed to keep us scrolling and checking in, addicted to the endorphin rush of an incoming email or the ping of a notification. They bank on us being mindless. Let's not be mindless. Let's take control of our time and our relationships, our self-image and our knowledge. Let's use technology as the intentional tool it should be—not the crutch it's become.

But sometimes I need to completely disconnect in order to regain that mindfulness. Sometimes I find myself just too deep down in the

Twitter

Texts

Calendar

Email

Software updates

TV

Facebook

Instagram

News Alert

Phone-free weekend

Unsubscribe

Delete apps and email

Go where Wi-Fi doesn't work

circuit-breakers

connected world to realize how far away from mindfulness I've drifted. Sometimes I need a circuit breaker.

TAKE A DIGITAL SABBATICAL

I've taken digital sabbaticals before, and while it's always a lot of work setting one up (prepping colleagues, clients, friends, and family for the fact that you will really, truly be off-line can be quite challenging), I have invariably come back having had a breakthrough of some sort.

Taking a long break—anywhere from a long weekend to many months—is an opportunity to let the stimulus slowly dissipate, revealing a whole other layer of thoughts and feelings that aren't given light when we're constantly connected. The added benefits of peace, creativity, and rest mean my productivity has always been much improved after a digital break.

GO OFF THE GRID

If you can't take a full sabbatical, perhaps head out of town for a few hours to somewhere you know has no internet reception, and revel in the peace it can bring. Even a few hours of uninterrupted off-line time are restorative in a way that surprises me. It makes me realize just how much I underestimate the energy cost of being constantly connected.

REMOVE APPS FROM THE PHONE

Sometimes I like to remove my email account from my phone (on a weekend away, for example), and I also like removing social media apps regularly. It gives me an opportunity to see just how many times a day my thumb drifts over to the app button without even thinking about it and how many times I'd find myself on Facebook or Instagram without realizing what I'd been doing.

Taking the apps off is a great circuit breaker and can lead to some unexpected changes. I removed the Facebook app from my phone for the Christmas break a few years ago and have never put it back on. I can only access Facebook via my browser now, which means I spend far less time scrolling through the holiday photos of someone I went to high school with and far more time doing things that are actually interesting!

○ ○ ○

These are all great ways to minimize the impact of technology on our lives, and adopting some of them will help us to get more work done, be more present, connect more in person, procrastinate less, and generally live a more intentional life.

But just like the person who has never spent time in nature won't bother fighting to protect something they don't value, you'll never fight for a disconnected life if you don't know how amazing it can be.

So do fun things in the real world. Hang out with your friends. Play a board game. Write a book. Create things rather than consume. Go watch a play. Look into the eyes of someone you think is wonderful. The more good stuff you fit into your disconnected life, the more time you'll want to spend off-line, enjoying those good things.

I never knew how amazing my off-line life could be, and I had no motivation to fight for it, not when my digital universe offered so many distractions. The real world was boring and difficult and pretty uncomfortable, so I stayed away from it as much as I could. I lived a hyperconnected, isolated life.

But now I disconnect in order to reconnect.

I disconnect in order to look directly at people, to remember I don't need to be available to everyone twenty-four hours a day.

I disconnect to tell stupid jokes with Ben and quote *Caddyshack* and talk about our plans and play pétanque and listen to music. To remember where we've come from and what we have ahead of us and to feel whole.

I disconnect in order to hold my daughter's hand and tell her stories and brush her cheek as she goes to sleep and never document those moments anywhere other than my own memory.

I disconnect to pay attention to my son's laughter and the way his nose scrunches up when I tickle him and how much he loves dinosaurs and the way he looks up at me like he believes in me. I

A modern day

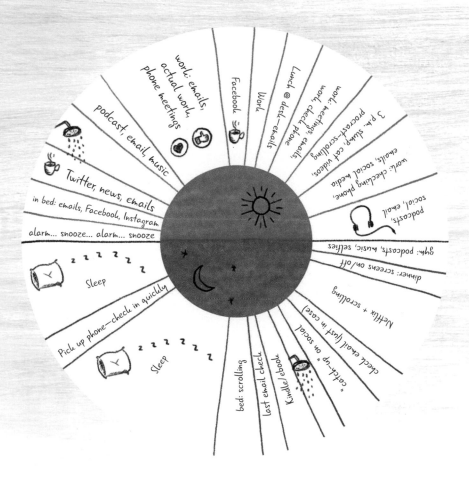

don't need a photo or a video to remember it. And I don't need an audience to validate it. Paying real attention and drinking in those moments imprints more on our brains and our hearts than taking a photo ever would.

The more I connect with people in real life, the more I have conversations and see their strengths, beauty, and imperfections, the more I realize we're all alike. We're all human. We're all trying. And the images we see online aren't the full picture; no matter how authentic the author, an Instagram post can't replace real connection.

So have a conversation and connect. Online posts aren't documentaries. They're a highlight reel. No one shows tantrums and arguments and dirty laundry and hangovers and bloated tummies and bad hair days unless it serves them to do so.

When you disconnect, use it as an opportunity to reconnect with something meaningful. Your breath, your thoughts, your emotions. The person next to you, the work you're doing, the reason you're doing it. Action, kindness, movement, purpose. Beauty, art, dirt, rocks, nature, stories. There is so much worth paying attention to in the here and now, and not all of it, not even most of it, can be fully experienced through a screen. The best you might get is a high-definition surrogate.

o o o

Can I paint a picture for you briefly as we consider the role of technology in slow living? It's currently 8:07 a.m. I'm sitting at the dining table of my parents' house, having skipped out on my family yesterday so I can finish this book. Since 5:00 a.m., these are the ways technology has impacted my life:

- I'm woken by birdsong on my iPhone. I've set my phone up to alert me at 8:45 p.m. that it's time to go to bed if I want to get a full eight hours of sleep. My alarm then goes off at 5:00 a.m., and birdsong is a nicer way to wake up than a blaring alarm.
- I get up, wash my face, get dressed, and go make a coffee.
- I pick up my coffee and my phone and go outside, where there is a gorgeous sunrise unfolding on what's going to be a hot January day. I know I need to get a lot of writing done today, so I Instagram my sunrise, let people know that I will be writing a lot today, and then go inside to start.
- I open an app that tracks my focus by growing an imaginary tree and set it for sixty minutes. If I pick up my phone before that sixty minutes is up, my imaginary tree dies. It seems stupid, but it's really helpful in stopping the mindless habit of picking up my phone when faced with something difficult.
- I sit at my computer and start writing. Thirty-five minutes in, I find myself stuck. This is normally when I would pick up my

phone, but knowing I have a fake tree growing, I sit and breathe deeply for a minute and then get back to writing.

- Once my tree alarm goes off, I make breakfast and scan my phone. Instagram likes, Facebook, Twitter, news websites. Ten minutes later, I realize I've been reading posts I don't care about. Instead, I go and inspect the snow forecast for Japan—we're due to fly out in four days.

- I call Ben and the kids and see how they're doing. Ben's already seen my Instagram post and knows I'm up and writing. He also knows I'm probably procrastinating like a champ.

- I get off the phone, make another coffee, and pick up my phone again. I'm aware that it's procrastination, and I don't do anything to stop it. I scan through my most visited websites again as a way of putting off the inevitable.

- I sit down, open my tree focus app, set the timer, and begin typing again.

As the day goes by, I will repeat these same processes many times over.

Technology has become a crutch I'm using to get through an uncomfortable experience. It's a way of putting off the work but still convincing myself I'm doing something worthwhile. Aside from talking to my family and harnessing technology to grow a pretend tree and limit my procrastination, none of that has been worthwhile. In this instance, technology is a distraction that is keeping me from feeling uncomfortable, from thinking too deeply, from doing too much.

The biggest culprits behind the endless scrolling:

- boredom
- procrastination
- emotional discomfort
- self-sabotage
- self-loathing or dissatisfaction
- habit
- looking for someone or something to inspire me

I don't share this to discount or invalidate the advice I've given up to this point but to illustrate just how easily connection technology can shift from useful to distracting, from helpful to detrimental. And as a reminder to, as always, pay attention to what we're doing and why we're doing it. To use it as a tool, not as a crutch.

(No lie: I just watched a video of a chameleon catching bubbles.)

six

A CABIN IN THE WOODS

If I asked you to think of a place you felt completely at ease, what would you see? Is it a house, a beach, a tree, or a river? Your office or a theater stage? What does this place look like? What can you hear? What smells and feelings does it evoke? What is it made of? Picture somewhere you feel completely safe and yourself. Somewhere that feels like home.

always picture a cabin in the woods. Not the Australian bush, but a deep, cool pine forest in the Canadian Rockies. There's a sloping forest floor covered in pine needles and the sound of distant birdsong. The surroundings don't always look exactly the same. Sometimes there's a lake. Sometimes it's summer. Sometimes it's evening. But most of the time, it's snowy, cold, quiet, and feels utterly like home. I don't know why this is my happy place, but it has been for a long time. I absolutely feel more at ease in the Canadian mountains than anywhere else in the world, but I've never been to a cabin in the woods. This is an imaginary place I've built over years.

My version of a slow life is in the construction of this cabin.

My Why is the foundation upon which everything else is built. The stronger I make my foundation, the fuller the cabin can become. And not full in a cluttered sense, but full of people, love, community, service, kindness, joy, dancing, parties, sorrow, presence. The stronger the foundation, the more it can hold.

The four walls of the cabin are made of timber and stone, earthy and timeless, a reminder to do better by what will remain once we're gone. These four walls are made of noticing and intention, mindfulness and connection.

Set in each of these walls are windows that look to the trees outside. These windows are time spent in nature, breathing fresh air, watching the stars and the moon, walking barefoot on the grass, and swimming in cold waters.

There is a front door that swings open, welcoming anyone who visits, inviting them into the space inside. The door is openness and honesty, kindness and joy, and it moves easily on its hinges. The walls support a high, strong roof of shingles that protects and cares for everything that's important to me. The environment, people, purpose. Caring more about the things that matter, shielding us from the things that don't.

The space within the cabin is warm, open, and airy. It's not big, but it's big enough, and it's been carved out by decluttering, learning to let go, saying no, and caring less about things that aren't important.

If this cabin—the foundation, walls, and roof—were all I ever built in my attempts to create a slow life, it would be an amazing thing. I could have so easily moved through life mindlessly, comfortably not noticing. Constantly looking for more, better, faster, shinier. Missing the beauty and the pain of a fully lived life.

I assumed that once I embraced a philosophy of less stuff and more mindfulness, a simpler, slower life would miraculously appear, and everything would be great. That once I identified my Why and began living in accordance with it, I'd be happy.

But what about the less significant things that impact the way I live every day? What about the actions and the choices that are significant but not important enough to appear in my eulogy? Where do they fit?

Apologies for the tortured metaphor here, but these are the things I furnish my cabin with. They're not essential to life, but they do make it better.

And what are these things?

They're both practical and centered on self-care. If I were to reach for another overused analogy, these are the equivalent of filling my own cup so I can fill the cups of others. They support my wellness, my soul, my heart, and my mind. When I use them, they allow me to be a stronger, better, kinder, healthier, more compassionate, more generous person, because they encourage well-being: mental, emotional, spiritual, physical.

I've struggled to write about these things, because first, I'm not an expert in any of them, and there are already enough people in the world pretending to have absolute answers where there are none. Second, they're all *self*-related, and over the past thirty-five years, I've absorbed the message that self-care is selfish.

But you know what? That's OK. In fact, selfishness? Bring it on. Because I've realized that in order to leave the world a better place than I found it—to be compassionate and caring—I need to be strong, I need to be vulnerable, I need to be healthy and vital and full of good stuff like kindness and generosity and laughter. Not because those things make me a Good Person but because if I have those things, I can turn around and share them. I can work hard and be kind and parent well and be a good friend and partner and daughter and sister. I can act on my desire to change the world, and I can do crazy things like write books full of weird analogies and have conversations with strangers across the globe.

My analogy cabin is the result of years of work—letting go of clutter and ownership, creating and maintaining space, learning to pay attention and live mindfully, practicing meditation and the art of noticing, disconnecting to reconnect, spending time outdoors, becoming mindful in my relationships—but the things discussed in the following sections have turned it from a building where I can exist to a home where I can truly live. I use some of them all the time, while others I dust off as needed. Some I'm quite good at putting to use, while others are less familiar, and I'm still working out where they're going to fit. I don't do any of them perfectly or even well necessarily, but I don't let that stop me anymore. If there's anything I've learned over the past few years, it's that a small, imperfect action every day is going to get me further than one big occasional change.

Sleep

I used to be a monstrous night owl, going to bed at two or three most mornings. When I was running the jewelry business, the middle of the night was the only time I could work for an extended period, so I would sit in the living room, hunched over a mobile workbench, back aching, eyes burning, unable to stop or to sleep.

Constructing a life of intention,
mindfulness, kindness, and peace
is something worth celebrating.

Once our second child was born, my sleep requirements shifted again, and I would take it however I could. It was never great quality, and I got used to living on only a few hours of broken sleep per night, but among those sleep-deprived days, I discovered something unexpected—I love the early morning hours. The quiet, the light, the coolness of our house as everyone else sleeps. There were years where I simply didn't get the opportunity to enjoy an early morning by myself because both our kids were accidental co-sleepers who would wake early and hungry, which I found challenging. But despite feeling like a century at the time, that era passed quickly, and early mornings have been a staple for me ever since.

The problem I had was in going to sleep early enough.

I enjoyed the early morning time, but it took me a while to realize that I needed to adjust the time I was going to sleep as well as the time I was getting up. And it wasn't until I realized I'd been existing on four to five hours of sleep per night, wondering why I was constantly snacking and mainlining coffee, that the penny dropped.

Instead of going to sleep at a reasonable time, I would lie in bed reading on my iPad for hours, my brain slowly waking up in the glare of the blue light, my legs twitching under the sheets, when I should have been drifting off to sleep.

Ben and I conducted two highly nonscientific month-long sleep experiments in 2016. The first, as I've already mentioned, saw us create a screen-free bedroom, while the second experiment had us do anything possible to get eight hours of sleep a night, which was two hours more than I was getting at the time. We wanted to see if there was an impact on both the quality and the ease with which we fell asleep, and if you'll pardon the pun, the difference was night and day.

Turns out my brain and body really did work better when I slept enough. I lost weight during the eight hours of sleep experiment, felt calmer, was more productive, read more books, and fell asleep much more rapidly. I woke refreshed and had so much more energy, and my mental clarity was amazing.

Fast-forward a year, and the changes remain. Our bedrooms are completely tech-free now (I keep my phone in another room and still use it as an alarm clock), and I regularly get between seven and eight hours of sleep. Granted, it doesn't always happen, but the fact that we prioritize sleep now is the biggest difference. Good sleep is as much of a nonnegotiable as good food now, where previously we used sleep as a bargaining chip, giving it up in order to fit more into our days.

Self-Talk

When I was about twelve, a very mean girl took up residence inside my head. She stuck around for many, many years, whispering bitter words to me, convincing me I wasn't good enough, causing me to question my abilities, my worth, my place in the world.

I would love to tell you that she moved on as I grew up, but the truth is, she's still here. She's much quieter now, and the venom in her voice no longer affects me as much as it used to, but this inner mean girl has been a doozy of a vocal companion all my life.

Listening to her vitriol, I've spent years feeling insecure, unlikeable, unlovable, unwanted, unworthy, unattractive, unmotivated, uneducated. Lacking in every way. Even in the face of outright opposition from others, it was obvious to me that I wasn't worthwhile. I was an imposter. A fake. Amazingly, it was an experiment in meditation that taught me how to put this inner mean girl in her box and give her the attention she deserves (which is very little).

During this month-long experiment, I discovered a loving kindness practice. In this guided meditation, I had to sit quietly and tell myself that I was loved, over and over again. I was required to say it and believe it before moving on to spreading that love to others. It felt foreign. Strange and sacred. It felt self-centered, and I liked it.

I don't know if it's a uniquely Australian thing to use self-love as an insult, but I heard it enough growing up to believe that loving myself was a conceited thing to do. "Oooh, she loves herself. Ugh."

Well, sorry, but yes, I guess I do.

I believe love and action will change the world and have always tried to bring that belief to everything I do. I'd always tried to convince myself that while I didn't always *like* a lot of people, I loved them as my brothers and sisters. But before I knew how to love myself, I'm not sure how effective I was in actually doing so. I came from a place of defensiveness and insecurity, reacting to the voice of my inner mean girl.

As I've learned to shut her down, I've started hearing a different voice—my own. And it's confident and assured. Not cocky, but convinced I have value. I couldn't write this book without that voice. I couldn't share without that voice. I couldn't love or give or parent wholly without that voice.

What's more, it's giving me the gift of gentleness. When the only voice I heard regularly was one of venom, spite, ill will, and delight at any perceived failings, it was impossible to be kind to myself. I couldn't grant compassion to myself. I couldn't acknowledge my strengths, only weaknesses. I couldn't give myself a pat on the back, only a kick in the ribs.

Now there is acceptance and kindness. A determination and a warmth. An ability to say, "Hey, I love you."

Gratitude

Gratitude is my antidote. An antidote to dissatisfaction, to complacency, to first-world complaints, to the blind spots of privilege. It's an antidote to the Be Happy Whens:

- I'll be happy when...I get a new client.
- I'll be happy when...the kids are older, and I'm sleeping through the night again.
- I'll be happy when...she asks me to move in.
- I'll be happy when...we've booked the trip.
- I'll be happy when...we get pregnant.

There are legitimate reasons to feel bereft in life, to feel bitter disappointment, sadness, pain, grief, or inconvenience. Practicing gratitude won't necessarily make those disappear, and I've never used it to mask negative feelings or pretend they're not there. Instead, practicing gratitude is recognizing that the hurt, disappointment, envy, or irritation isn't all there is. There is more, and there is always something to be grateful for.

Every moment of every day, I can find something to be disappointed by. I can look around me at any given second and find something that is lacking. Something not quite right. Something to complain about, or feel annoyed by, or offended by, or saddened by. Instead, I try to flip it. If there is always something to grumble about, surely there's also something to be grateful for in this same situation? My breath, my heartbeat, the sunshine, the clothes I wear, the people around me, the peace of this country, the freedoms we have, the glimmer of hope. There is always something, no matter how dark the day, and that realization makes me feel light and spacious.

There is a claustrophobic feeling that comes from the Be Happy Whens, and it's a feeling I used to wrap myself in constantly. It came from the secret knowledge that it wouldn't ever be enough. No matter how much I tried to convince myself that the thing I really wanted was the last thing ever, I knew it wouldn't be long before I wanted something else. It was a never-ending cycle.

The lightness I feel when I acknowledge that right here, right now is enough, is a letting go. It's contentment born of gratitude.

Contentment

I used to think of contentment as the underachieving cousin of happiness. It was mediocre, average, and dull. Why stop at contentment when I could aim for happiness? Joy? Ecstasy?

But where can I go from there?

Striving for constant happiness was a denial of so many important feelings, and by embracing instant gratification and the ever-striving attempts at joy, I was diving headfirst into consumption, comparisons, entitlement, and the race to keep up with those ever-present but never real Joneses.

Contentment is a quiet acceptance, a peacefulness, a calm amid the endless wanting. When I choose contentment, there's no competition with anyone. The race to keep up simply disappears. Once I realized this, I gave myself permission to see and accept things as they were—myself included. No constant striving meant the person, place, experience, or relationship was enough. Right here, right now, it's enough.

I still crave change. I still work toward improvement. Contentment simply brings slowness to those changes. It brings quality, not quantity. Depth, not superficiality. It brings peace.

Reading

Without a book, I'm lost.

Sometimes the books are nonfiction, sometimes they're work related, but mostly, they're fiction. They're big stories about fascinating people, and they're small stories of flawed humans. They're often apocalyptic, and they all transport me to a world of my own imagining.

What exactly does this have to do with slow living? It's relevant because I make time for reading when there really isn't any time to be had. When I'm spent and burnt out and I can't muster the wherewithal to meditate or do five minutes of yoga or make a green smoothie, I will always make time to dive into a book.

I was always a voracious reader as a kid, using it as an escape. I remember going to the dentist when I was maybe nine years old and had one of those slimy, tangy fluoride gels applied to my teeth. I wasn't allowed to rinse my mouth for thirty minutes afterward, so I sat in the car, clenching my teeth in an attempt to keep the vomitous flavor from touching my taste buds. Once we'd pulled into our driveway at home, I sat in the car reading my Baby-Sitters Club book while trying not to think about my mouth. Eventually, I slipped into another world and sat there for three hours. Books have always been an escape pod from bad days and dentist appointments.

In the worst of my depression, I didn't read books at all. I simply never made time to read for enjoyment. I would read about how to improve my business ("Six Steps to a Six-Figure Income from Your Handmade Business!"). I'd read case studies of successful people ("This Woman Has Seventeen Children, a Multimillion Dollar Company, and Six-Pack Abs!"). I'd read glossy magazines and be filled with shame ("All You Need to Know About Getting a Thigh Gap!"). I'd read street fashion blogs and feel frumpy ("Cute Shoes But That Blouse Makes Her Look Like—Ugh—a Suburban Mom"). I would read and compare. I would read and berate. I would read and tear myself to shreds. But I would never read for fun.

Then one day I picked up a copy of *The Hunger Games*. Uplifting, right? I read all three of those books in four days. I inhaled that story like life itself. I ignored work. I ignored cleaning. I ignored my own misery. Every possible moment, I read. We ate baked beans on toast because I was too engrossed to cook. I drank tea and stayed up late as I fell in love with a world that wasn't mine. The pain wasn't mine. I barely slept, but I was electrified.

Is *The Hunger Games* the best book series ever? Not necessarily. But I didn't care, because it came alive for me, and I remembered what it was like to be lost in the world of my own vision. To sit in the darkening car, reading the Baby-Sitters Club books. The words weren't mine, but the images in my mind's eye were. I was captive. I was mindful. I was both completely present and totally absent.

Now I make time to read. I'll go to bed at the same time as the kids just so I get to read more. I sit on the grass for ten minutes and read as I eat my lunch. When Ben watches some form of sportsball (go… team!), I read. I read in the bath. I read waiting for the doctor. I read with my kids. I read every day. Even if it's only one page before I fall asleep, I always make time for a story.

It's taught me about words and building worlds and what it is to be human, but it's also taught me that I will find time for things I'm passionate about. And it repays me tenfold every time.

Food

I used to have a very fraught relationship with food. There was a love-hate thing going on, and while I didn't really struggle with weight, I struggled with health.

Because I didn't have strategies for dealing with listlessness, boredom, or procrastination, food was how I dealt with those feelings. It's how I dealt with stress and uncertainty. It's how I passed the time. And I ate mindlessly, choosing whatever my cravings told me to. Chocolate. Junk food. Takeout. Way too much of the good stuff like delicious cheese and wine. Lots of high-sugar, energy-promising processed snacks. This is what my cravings told me I needed because I was exhausted, or stressed, or sad, or relieved, or happy. Every emotion had food attached, and none of it was kale.

Around the same time as I discovered mindfulness, I began to pay attention to the way nutritious, whole food made me feel. I'd love to say there was an immediate turnaround, but as you already know, I'm not a quick study, and I've always been a fan of self-sabotage. I would tie my thoughts of food to the notion of good and bad, and I would tie my identity to that goodness or badness every day. It never ended well.

Ben and I did a month-long sugar-free experiment, which was the turning point for me. I'd already made changes by gradually cutting out soft drinks, processed and chocolatey snacks, and sugary booze, eating more veggies, and drinking a killer green smoothie most days. And I'd seen gradual but unmistakable improvements in energy, stamina, and my overall health. But it wasn't until we challenged ourselves to completely reexamine our food habits that I recognized just how much

of an emotional eater I was. Cutting out the thing that made me inclined to binge (sugar) and replacing it with food that actually satisfied me (whole foods, lots of veggies, good fats), I was able to break the cycle and haven't looked back.

The slow food philosophy of seasonal, whole, quality produce is one we stick to closely now. We cook every night except Fridays when we eat pizza (and it's amazing), and we don't really do processed snack food. Our kids are slowly learning that junk food is junk fuel and that we're not going to feed them that stuff.

I know how easy it is to become overwhelmed by the all-or-nothing mentality, and I am a big fan of moderation. I happily bake, we eat good-quality dark chocolate, we love our Friday night pizza, and I don't feel bad about any of it. But once I recalibrated my taste buds and my relationship with food, I was released from eating emotionally, and old habits didn't so much die hard as simply fizzle out in an unappetizing puff of smoke.

It's only when I am stressed that I find myself backsliding into those old habits, and the fact that I now pay close attention and am aware of my patterns means it never gets too far out of hand. Plus, the "treats" that used to be so tempting and delicious don't satisfy like they once did.

Bottom line: we eat more nutritious whole foods and use them to crowd out the unsatisfying processed stuff.

Movement

This is an area of life I am still learning to accommodate, but being physically active has proven so vital to my well-being, I couldn't not mention it. I love slacklining, hiking, snowboarding, running, dancing, and yoga, and I try to add as much movement to my day as possible. Rather than force myself to the gym regularly, I try to make room for incidental exercise as opposed to hardcore cardio.

I wake up and practice yoga most mornings. Sometimes that's five minutes while I make a cup of tea; sometimes it's a vinyasa that runs for thirty minutes. I often set a timer for every half hour during the workday and break up all the sitting with stretches, planks, headstands, and walks around the garden. I'll take the kids on a short hike in the afternoon, or sometimes we go indoor rock climbing. Twice a week, Ben and I go to a yoga class together, and I like walking the kids to the school in the mornings when time allows. I dance around the house when I'm cleaning (much to the embarrassment of anyone who's ever seen it), and a little bit of gardening is part of most mornings—usually I'm meant to be hanging out the laundry.

I do all these things for how they make me feel, rather than how they make me look. I've discovered movement I love, and when it's incidental and spread throughout the day, it simply becomes part of my rhythm.

Travel

I was lucky enough to travel a lot as a kid. My mom and dad took us to Fiji and the United States when we were young, and I have fond memories of spending time with my sisters and parents, exploring new places, visiting Disneyland, hearing different accents, seeing places I'd only ever seen on TV.

But it wasn't until Ben and I took off for a year-long backpacking adventure that I really fell in love with traveling. It's a fairly terrible cliché, but I began to discover myself as we traveled. I existed not as someone's daughter or friend, but as me. And I watched as the world opened up, offering me choices, introducing me to people and places outside my little bubble of existence.

The more we've let go, the more my nomadic spirit emerges. A house full of stuff, a calendar full of commitments, a credit card full of debt—these things are heavy and made travel and exploring feel out of reach. Now, we feel free to wander. It doesn't need to be a big, expensive overseas vacation—we love camping or going to a new beach. It's more about the pace with which we do it.

We use travel, in all its forms, as a time to connect with each other, different cultures, new experiences, and a slower pace. We tend to stay in one place rather than move around, and while that might seem like a wasted opportunity to see more, we tend to go

deep rather than wide, and as a result, we walk away feeling like we've discovered something we might not have otherwise.

We also love spending time in communities rather than resorts or vacation destinations. We visit playgrounds and coffee shops and pubs. I love visiting local libraries, community centers, markets, and independent bookshops. Going deep into a place doesn't require a passport or a long period of time, rather a willingness to see fewer places but see more of the places you go.

○ ○ ○

I'm not going to tell you that all the things listed in this chapter will work for you, and I'm not going to tell you how they should look in your life. What I can tell you is that as I gradually learn to pay attention to each of these elements of my life, there are incremental improvements. Some make me uncomfortable. Some I do not love. Some stick. Some come and go. But paying attention to them is a game changer. Just noticing, getting curious, experimenting, and seeing how I feel. Asking how I feel. Asking if it's going to create more of my Why or less. More peace or more comparison. More abundance or more scarcity. More health or less.

It's a pretty nice cabin, eh?

Pay attention to how movement makes
you feel—not how it makes you look.
Use it to fill you up, not deplete you.

seven

WOBBLY BALANCE

As I moved through the gradual and messy process of slowing down, the question I was asking myself was the same one so many people have asked me over the years: life is already too busy, how am I supposed to find time for slowing down? If I'm already struggling to do all the things required of me every day, isn't "slow down" just another item on my to-do list? Another way to make me feel guilty for not doing enough?

W hat they're really saying is this: I'm reading these suggestions, and I get it, but how do I find the time for any of
it? How do I keep all the balls in the air and still make
space for slow?

You don't.

Simply put, you stop trying to juggle all the balls all the time.

When I finally asked the question of "How?" I didn't understand the
answer that came back to me. What do you mean, I don't have to juggle
all the balls? Are you mad? How can I prove to people that I'm Doing
Well if I don't have all the balls in the air? How will I get things done?

It took me a while to accept, but it turns out that this really is a very
simple answer. Stop trying to do it all perfectly, and instead embrace a
wobbly kind of balance.

I used to imagine balance as a two-legged stool. One leg was work,
and the other was life. These two legs needed equal attention and equal
weight in order for the stool to remain upright and stable. If life got too
much time, the stool tipped over. If the work side was too heavy, everything fell apart.

Can you imagine how much energy goes into staying up on that
stool? How hard you need to work simply to keep the weight evenly
balanced and the seat upright? Let alone the glaring issue that work
and life cannot be so easily separated, nor are they the only two legs on
which a full life stands.

One Mother's Day, Ben and the kids gave me a slackline. It's a two-inch-wide length of nylon webbing, like a flattened-out tightrope, strung between two points. Ours is about thirty feet long and hangs a foot off the ground, pulled tautly between two trees in our backyard.

The idea is to walk along its length—balancing, turning, jumping, or even doing yoga on the line. It's so much fun and an amazing core strengthener but much harder than I thought it would be.

As I raise myself up on to the shaking line, as I put one foot in front of the other, as I take careful steps along the rope, every muscle is taut, trying desperately not to over- or undercompensate. My mind is focused and singular in its attention. My sights need to be set on a specific spot and not move at all; otherwise, I'll fall.

Ten minutes spent trying to remain balanced on a slackline is exhausting (and fun) and makes me realize that if balancing on a line for just ten minutes is so tiring when there's nothing more important than ego up for grabs, I was delusional to think I could keep a busy, full life perfectly balanced and not struggle under the pressure.

For years, balance looked like perfection. Everything in its place, evenly weighted, everyone happy, and everything correct.

balance / ˈbæləns / noun

an even distribution of weight enabling someone or something to remain upright and steady.

Upright and steady. Not a wobble in sight.

I subscribed wholeheartedly to the myth of work/life balance, where we somehow managed to eke out an equality of time and energy across all major areas of life—work, family, health, friends, community, spirituality...

I'd convinced myself that if I just worked hard enough, said yes enough, compared myself harshly enough, and beat myself up enough, I would achieve it. And somehow the exhaustion, the discontent, the comparisons, the guilt, the shoulds would simply disappear when I reached this nirvana of a balanced life.

That's what I was striving for as I stayed up late every night, desperately trying to right the imbalance between parenting and me time. That's why I was aiming to improve the balance between comfort food and health as I forced myself to the gym every morning, in spite of the fact that lifting weights and doing an hour of cardio left me completely exhausted. That's what I was looking for as I tried desperately to be everything to everyone, all the time.

I was striving for perfection, running full-pace toward a mirage, killing myself trying to get closer to a life of balance, where everything is as it should be. Evenly and constantly balanced.

On a slackline, that kind of balance is helpful. In life, it's damaging and exhausting.

Deep inside, I'm a contrarian brat, so once I'd decided that work/life balance wasn't sustainable, I threw myself wholly into imbalance—an unsustainable workload, a health kick, or particular parenting goals—not even trying to be intentional about it, as though my inevitable burnout was proving some kind of point. Now I can see that the idea of balance is a good one, when viewed with two caveats:

1. Not everything in our lives deserves the same weight. Aim instead for the correct weight.
2. Balance isn't a daily act. Not everything will be given attention every day, and that's OK.

The difference is in the weight we give things. Keeping the house immaculately clean doesn't need or deserve the same weight as spending time with our closest people. We know this, but the myth of balance tells us otherwise. It keeps us perched on the wavering tightrope, terrified of falling too far into imbalance. Because we know an imbalanced person isn't stable. They're not succeeding or adulting or kicking goals or coping. And we don't want to be one of those people.

So we balance. We exhaust ourselves. We're never fully in a moment, because we're worried about all the other areas of life that aren't getting our attention in that moment. We've turned balance into a constant struggle rather than a long game.

I no longer strive for balance every morning. I don't berate myself when things are heavily weighted to work, or family, or downtime, or health, because there are other seasons in life where I'm heavily weighted in another direction. And when I look back over the past twelve months, I feel balanced and content, in spite of the fact that I've worked more hours this past year than ever before. In spite of the fact that there were days our kids watched too much TV. In spite of the fact that sometimes breakfast for dinner was a thing we did. In spite of the fact that I chose to sleep in rather than get up for yoga.

And that's because I've discovered long-term balance. Working some nights means we keep most weekends free and find time for a hike some afternoons. Letting the kids watch too much TV on the occasional weekend is balanced out by the fact that they never watch it during the week. Breakfast for dinner is a novelty that means everyone is happy and fed, and when I have a deadline looming, it's a price well worth paying. Hitting snooze and skipping yoga is worthwhile, because I can see that an hour more sleep is necessary given the late night I had.

These choices are intentional. Brooke of old would have berated herself brutally for any or all of these decisions. I used to believe that I could do everything and be everywhere. I could work longer hours, make the deadline, cook the delicious and nutritious meal, play with the kids, get enough sleep, and focus on my health. And I absolutely can do all those things. But not at the same time. Not on the same day.

Realizing that was a delightful freedom. Letting go of that notion of constant balance was releasing a breath I didn't realize I'd been holding.

You mean I don't have to be everything to everyone all the time? I don't have to keep all the balls in the air all the time? I can change balls? I can choose different balls? (I wish there was another way to say that without using "balls" so many times. Actually…never mind.)

Balance is finding the correct weight for every area of life and understanding that the correctness of that weight will change over time. Balance is fluid and flexible. Balance is alive and aware. Balance is intention.

Now, that's a definition I can get behind.

This idea of balance—a correctness rather than an equalness, an agency as opposed to a prescription—has taught me some of the most important lessons of my life:

- I cannot be everything to everyone.
- I cannot be in all places at once.
- Saying yes to one thing means saying no to another.
- Saying no to one thing means I can say yes to another.
- Perfection doesn't exist. Let it go.
- I cannot change people.

- I have to stop comparing myself to others. They aren't me. I'm not them.
- I will never finish the laundry. (Unless we all embrace full-time nudity.*)
- I can't control everything.
- Bad things happen to good people and vice versa.
- My kids aren't me.
- Being all in a moment means I'm all out of another.
- Envy and jealousy are different things.
- Achievements never look like I thought they were going to.
- Being kind to others is addictive.
- Being kind to myself is addictive.
- I can't always be self-possessed.
- Sometimes I need a cheerleader.
- I like being part of a community.
- Asking for help is hard but necessary.

Now this idea of balance is all well and good. It's another idea that most of us can agree has some merit. But how does it fit into life in a practical way? How can you give things their correct weight? How do you find your own version of wobbly balance? And what's more, how

---

* Note to self: research benefits of full-time nudity.

can you make that work in your day-to-day life? You know, the full and busy one?

Much like decluttering or learning to practice mindfulness, there are a multitude of ways to embrace wobbly balance.

Not all of them will apply all the time, but each of these ideas has made an impact in my life, bringing me a sense of contentment and long-term balance, whereas old ideas of perfection left me exhausted and dissatisfied with my efforts.

Learn to Tilt

Tilting is the opposite of constant balance. It's willingly pouring my attention into an area that needs it (or the area I need) and acknowledging that I will be tilting away from other parts of life—into meditation, into creativity, into play, into noticing, into people, into a good book. Away from doing, planning, list making, screens, comparisons. In an earlier book, *Destination Simple*, I took a deep dive into the importance of tilting (I'd encourage you to take a look if you haven't already), and when I realized that tilting gave me permission to let go of perfection, I felt free.

Go Deep Instead of Shallow

Being completely in a moment—drinking in the details, the people, the sensations—fills me up in ways that phoning it in never can. Like eating a nutritious, home-cooked meal versus eating junk food—one leaves you satisfied with less; the other leaves you hungry and looking for more.

Learning to be fully present brings so much depth, which carries so much more weight than going through the motions ever could. Just one hour of true quality time with my family—talking, walking, playing, listening, no distractions, no half-assing it—counts for so much more than an entire day spent existing next to each other, playing with our screens of choice, semi-listening to what each other has to say.

Make Time for What's Truly Important

We each have twenty-four hours in a day, and when I began looking at how I chose to spend those twenty-four hours, it became clear that not all action was created equal.

I wanted to work more effectively in order to have more time for my family, so why was I spending hours flicking through my social media accounts? I wanted to eat a great breakfast every morning, so why was I hitting snooze on the alarm after watching one too many Netflix shows the night before? I craved quality time with Ben, so why did we fill our weekends with extra commitments and housework?

By paying attention to my time, I began to see there really was room for the important things; I just wasn't spending my time there. So I began to weigh up the mindless scrolling against productive work, snoozing against breakfast, quality time versus busyness. I began to take responsibility for my time and how it was spent. Once I realized I had a choice, it was simpler (though not always easier) to spend it more wisely.

This is advice we often don't want to hear, because we're convinced the scrolling, emailing, endless tidying, and busy work is important. We enjoy telling others we're busy. Too busy, in fact, for things that are important to us, and isn't that a shame? But can I *honestly* say my priority is eating better if I have enough time to scroll aimlessly through social media and clickbait for an hour but not enough time to cook?

Nominate one area of life you know is getting too much time, and simply monitor it for a few days. You might be shocked to learn how much time you spend on social media, or how often you check emails without actually responding, or how many minutes a day are spent in meetings you don't need to attend. That's time you could be spending on the things you really value, so start viewing it as a yes/no. Yes to cooking, no to mindless scrolling. Yes to more sleep, no to Netflix. Yes to efficient work, no to Facebook procrastination.

Procrastinate Less

There's a good reason I included procrastination in the previous paragraph. I could procrastinate for Australia and win a gold medal at that, so I have needed to make a huge and gradual shift in order to limit time spent in dawdling limbo.

To get out of the habit of procrastination, I had to find clarity on what it was I was trying to do. "Write a chapter of my book" wasn't helpful. It offered too many opportunities to lose focus and drift off into a daydream. "Write five hundred words of the third chapter of the book" is pretty good. "Write five hundred words of the third chapter of the book, following this preplanned structure" is even better.

Then it's simply a matter of doing the work. There is no other way. But instead of focusing on the entire task, I focus on the stupidly easy first step of the task. Rather than focus on all five hundred words I need to write, I instruct myself to sit down and open my document. Instead of commanding myself to go for a thirty-minute run, I tell myself to put on my shoes, walk out the front door, and close it behind me. I'm on my way and would feel ridiculous turning around and going back inside.

Once the task is underway, momentum takes over, and procrastination becomes an annoyance rather than a constant obstacle.

The other really important part of this is to focus on one thing at a time. If we attempt to start decluttering the house and practicing mindfulness and sleeping more and meditating and drinking green smoothies on one day, of course we're going to procrastinate, because where do we start?

Get clear on the first step, and give it time.

Get Organized (to a Point)

I always thought being organized was at odds with slow living, because I assumed *slow* was a blissed-out state of not needing to worry. If you lived a slow life, you somehow didn't need to pay bills or get up to an alarm or make sure the kids had costumes ready for the school performance. I know now, and hopefully you do too, that this is not the case. Slow living is about intention, spending more time on things that are important and less on things that aren't. Getting organized (enough) is a way to do more of the important and less of the unimportant.

Being organized is great. Rigidity, however, can be problematic. Knowing what's ahead is helpful. Being tied to a rock-solid schedule is less helpful in trying to find wobbly balance, because we don't have anywhere to go if we need to flex or change. Take the time to establish a rhythm to your days, your weeks, and your seasons—one that works for you. Once you've established that rhythm, you can move through your day knowing things will happen, and if they don't, they'll happen the next day. Establishing an effective rhythm removes a lot of the headwork of trying to be organized and allows a freedom to speed up or slow down as needed.

What does this actually look like in practical terms?

I've worked out the tasks that need to happen each week and nominated a day for them to be done. This was planned out for a reason, so I don't feel the need to second-guess it each week and now simply let that rhythm unfold each day, knowing it can change if necessary. For example, I've allowed time for yoga and meditation every morning, but occasionally I'll stay up later than normal, and I'll skip my morning practice. This isn't so much a matter of laziness but rather a choice to tilt into getting the sleep I need, which, as a nod to self-care, I'm more than OK with.

I'm not a particularly organized person and am still likely to leave things to the last minute. But becoming an organized (enough) person has made me more efficient, more productive, more satisfied, and more confident. Knowing I won't be caught out, knowing things aren't going to get too out of control, means I can move through my tasks as best as I can and leave it at that—as imperfect as it looks most of the time. Plus, keeping up on tasks means they actually take less time overall. The kitchen only takes twenty minutes to clean each week as opposed to the deep clean it would require if only done occasionally.

Instead of focusing on the entire task—even if it's small—try focusing on the tiniest first step you can think of. Instead of finishing your assignment, pick up your pen and open your notebook. Instead of tidying the whole garden bed, go outside and pull one weed. Instead of assembling an entire LEGO set with your kids, open the instructions and find the first three pieces.

Drop Your Standards (to a Point)

If your standards are high (hovering somewhere around perfection, perhaps) it's very easy to never be satisfied with your performance, whether it's work, parenting, being a good friend, keeping house, or nailing your crow pose. When you get sick or have to work late or spend longer chatting to your neighbor, it's easy to beat yourself up over the skipped yoga class or leftovers for dinner. But by embracing the *ish*, dropping standards just a little, letting go of the all-or-nothing mentality, you can accept that sometimes life just happens that way, and there's no need to feel like a failure.

What this dropping of standards will look like to you is highly individual, but for me, it's:

- no more ironing (I used to spend hours ironing everything from tea towels to tiny baby clothes)
- being OK if the bathroom or kitchen isn't cleaned to a brilliant shine every week
- planning for leftovers every week and cooking simple, easy meals instead of complicated dishes
- opting for done rather than perfect

It's not about laziness or becoming slovenly but rather acknowledging that sometimes, close-ish is good enough-ish.

Let Go of Guilt (to a Point)

I used to revel in guilt, secretly loving that it gave me ammunition to hate myself viciously at every turn for my failure to be everything to everyone at every moment. This kind of guilt is horribly detrimental, a vicious cycle of expectation and failure. In order to embrace a wobbly balance, we need to let go of this kind of guilt and move on.

On the other hand, guilt can also be helpful in drawing our attention to areas of life we value but which have become neglected. There is a particular pang in the gut that will let us know if we're consistently making choices that move us further from our Why or acting in a way that opposes our values.

This can feel like a guilt trip, another thing to beat ourselves up over, but if we get a pang when we think about an overdue phone call to our best friend, time spent with our loved ones, moving our body, or getting more sleep, we need to pay attention and ask if it's something we need to change or let go of.

Go Fast to Go Slow

Just like wobbly balance asks us to give things the *correct* weight rather than equal weight, slow living asks us to give our days and tasks the correct pace. And sometimes that correct pace is fast.

Going fast allows me to go slow. I work hard to get things done in order to give myself time for slow. In fact, I really like the adrenaline rush of a tight deadline. But when the adrenaline rush or tight deadline or busy period expands to become the norm, I know I've shifted from right-paced to hectic.

Like everything else I've spoken about in this book, the key is intention. Am I working hard in service of my Why? Or am I working hard simply because I think I should? Has adrenaline-fueled and frantic become the new normal? That's not going fast to go slow. That's when I've tipped into living a hectic life.

Go Slow to Go Fast

Conversely, we also need to go slow if we want to go fast. Going slow doesn't need to be a snail's pace meander through the countryside, and it doesn't need to be a day spent doing nothing (although both sound delightful to me!).

In those times of intentional slow lie rejuvenation, rest, depth, and quality time. It's not necessary or possible to go slow all the time, just like it's not possible to go fast all the time—it's all about finding that wobbly balance.

To me, going slow to go fast looks like tiny pockets of mindfulness, regular meditation, a consistent yoga practice, single tasking, quality time with my loved ones, and gratitude, which then deliver me the energy, margin, and buffer to go fast when necessary.

Embrace Different Seasons

There will be seasons in life that feel too busy, too full, too complex, and sometimes even too difficult. Starting a new job, welcoming a new baby, moving to a new place, or working on a big project are all things that can lead to a season of busyness. That's OK. It happens. As mindful and intentional as we are, these periods of busyness simply unfold sometimes.

Rather than rail against the busy season, wondering where you went wrong, it's important to embrace it with the knowledge that you will balance these seasons of busyness with seasons of less as you work toward long-term balance. And if your busy season is in service of your Why, moving you closer to living a values-based life, the discomfort can be worthwhile. It also highlights the beauty of a deliciously slow period when compared to a fast one.

Simple ways I keep organized (enough) at home:

- Everything has its place, making it easier to pack things away as needed.
- Particular days are assigned particular tasks (e.g., the bathrooms are cleaned on a Thursday, and the kitchen is cleaned on a Monday).
- I've let go of perfection, aiming instead for "good enough."
- Everyone pitches in and has responsibility for their own tasks.
- I embrace Gretchen Rubin's "One Minute Rule." If something is going to take less than a minute to do (send an email, make a phone call, put away the laundry), it gets done straightaway.
- We have a seasonal rhythm for bigger tasks, such as decluttering clothes and toys each school holiday, which means such things never become massively overwhelming jobs but regularly repeated, simple tasks that are quick, easy, and relatively painless.

Simple ways I keep organized (enough) at work:

- We hold a WIP (work in progress) meeting every Monday and outline tasks for the coming week, how long they will take, what days they are going to be completed, and what other events, appointments, or meetings are happening.
- I utilize my phone's calendar and add every event, meeting, phone call, school event, or appointment to it, with an alert set for the day before and an hour before the event.
- I update my to-do list every day and have only three main tasks for each day. If I get those three tasks completed, then I move on to other tasks.
- I don't worry about maintaining things like Inbox Zero every day or having a spotless desktop.
- I choose imperfect, small actions over perfect every day. It moves us forward and means that more gets done.

Bring Everything Back to Your Why

Let's go back to the slackline for just a minute, because I think there's a thread there I haven't fully unraveled, and it's one worth paying attention to.

When I'm balancing on the slackline, even though I mostly flap my arms and kick my legs around like a frog in a sock, I occasionally find a moment of perfect balance where I've lucked into a position that means my legs, arms, torso, and head are all perfectly balanced. It feels surreal, trancelike, and it's always fleeting. Things are always flexing and changing, and I never hold that precarious balance for long, because undoubtedly, something will change within seconds. I might shift my gaze or want to move into another position. I could have a tickle in my nose, or the kids might call my name. That perfect state of rigid balance is nice enough, but I know it's not real. I know it's not sustainable.

There is only one thing that brings a sense of sustainable balance while I'm on the line, and funnily enough, it doesn't look as composed as that precarious statue-like position I occasionally fluke. It's fairly inelegant and wobbles a lot more, but it lets me move and change positions freely. It allows me to walk up and down the line, turn myself around, balance on one leg, and generally have a lot more fun. So what is that one thing? My core.

I can get up on the line without engaging my core, and I can even manage a few moves without it. But it's not sustainable, it's not strong, and I can only rely on flailing or luck for a little while before I get tired and have to step off.

But when I engage my core, the muscles deep in my center that keep everything pulled in and solid, I can relax the rest of me just a little. Balancing on the line doesn't feel nearly as exhausting when I manage to engage my core (and let's be honest, after two kids, it's a little tougher than it used to be—both literally and metaphorically). It's still hard work to find balance, but the wobbly balance I achieve comes from a strong place rather than a frantic, tiring attempt to stay up.

So the question is, in trying to find a realistic approach to living a balanced life, what is your core? What is at the center of your life? What makes you feel solid and strong? When it's engaged, what makes you feel relaxed? Is it family? Creativity? Friends? Community?

I can assure you that none of the peripheral stuff—the clothes you wear, the car you drive, the throw cushions you covet—makes up your core. None of that stuff will help you to feel more balanced.

In fact, if you throw too much weight behind those things that don't matter, you might find yourself struggling to retain any kind of balance at all.

What does a (realistically) ideal day look like for you? One that fills you up, ticks the boxes you want ticked, makes time for the important things in your life, leaving you satisfied as you lie in bed at night? Not a holiday or a day off, but a work-school-cooking-meetings-laundry kind of a day.

What time do you get up? What's the first thing you do in the morning? What's something you do that's just for you? What do you eat for breakfast? How long does it take you to get ready for the day? What time do you leave? What's the first thing you do at the office? What's your attitude? What do you eat for lunch? When do you exercise? Which people do you spend time with? Do you listen to music? Will you have time to read a book? What's the state of your desk at the end of the day?

Think it through, and write it down if you want to. Choose one thing in that ideal day that you aren't currently doing—make it a good one, one that will contribute to your core—and add it to tomorrow. Make space for it. Tell yourself it's important. Tell yourself it's a core strengthener. Tell yourself it's going to improve your balance. Then actually do it.

○ ○ ○

By slowly strengthening your core, building it up with the things that are truly important, you will gradually become better at achieving wobbly balance. Your core will hold you in good stead as things shift and change, and you won't need to find that perfect, upright, constantly

My core strengtheners

What do you want at the center of your life? What fills you up? What makes you strong? Write these things down, and keep them in mind every time you look for balance (no matter how wobbly).

_____

_____

_____

_____

_____

_____

_____

slackline

stressed kind of balance. Instead, you'll have a flexibility and a fluidity to your days that allow for efficiency, compassion, productivity, and satisfaction, as well as a long-term balance that leaves you more content than any strained vision of work/life balance ever could.

eight

THE ART OF THE BACKSLIDE

So often, we avoid doing things because we're afraid. Afraid to fail, fall flat on our faces, or admit we made a mistake. Afraid to backtrack, afraid to be judged. We don't make changes, because we're afraid the requirements will exceed our capabilities or the problems will be bigger and more complex than we anticipated. So we stay where we are. Comfortably stuck. Studiously avoiding change or new experiences, out of fear of what the other side holds.

L et me set your mind at ease and relieve you of that fear right now. In choosing to wander down this slow road, to recalibrate the pace at which you live your life, at some point, you will stumble. You may steer away from your Why, you may go shopping when you don't need to, you may take on too many responsibilities, you may opt for convenience, you may lose sight of mindfulness, you may cram and rush and, eventually, lament. And you know what? It's OK.

Sometimes the *life* part of slow living gets in the way. Sometimes you will backslide. It might happen if you stop paying attention or when there's a change or addition to your life. If you move into a new house, get a dog, get married, break up, lose a loved one, start a new job, take on a new project, or any multitude of other changes, it can be easy to slide into those old, well-worn tracks of habit and behavior.

The art of the backslide is one I'm familiar with. Despite all best intentions, there have been days where I've felt completely overwhelmed, where it seemed easier to drift back into those well-worn tracks than to persevere down the newer, slower, more intentional path.

I don't tell you this to deflate your enthusiasm or to allow myself a great leaping dive into cynicism. I tell you this because there is a delicious liberation in acknowledging that our efforts will be imperfect, embracing it, and moving forward anyway, in understanding that there will be missteps along the way and to start walking in spite of them.

I will say, however, it's important to know there is a world of difference between a full-fledged burnout and a period of busyness.

I've been through both—thankfully, one much more than the other—and I've discovered that the shift into burnout can be deceptively gentle. Gradual and virtually undetectable, it can begin with a loss of focus, maybe a few too many yeses, a momentary loss of my Why, until I find myself curled up on the lounge, empty and exhausted.

Compare that to the period of life I'm in right now—it's a study in wobbly balance if ever I've seen one and totally different to burnout. I'm wrapping up the final pages of this book after working big days over the New Year break. My workload has been much higher than normal, and it's limited the amount of time I could spend with my family. But when we're together, I've worked to be fully present rather than distracted. I've kept to my daily yoga practice but reduced it to five-minute flows during writing breaks. There's laundry being ignored and less gardening being done, but it's enough for now. Because, as I've learned through embracing wobbly balance, I can't do it all at the same time. I'm still reading at night, still drinking lots of water, still feeling aware and mindful, still doing enough to maintain that balance. It's just more wobbly than usual. And that's OK.

And I think that's the difference between a burnout-inducing state of unsustainable busyness and a sustainable, albeit tiring, one: intention. The busy period I'm in now has an end date and a very clear purpose;

we knew it was coming, and we planned accordingly. The workload and the hours and the uber-tilting isn't forever, and it's very intentionally moving us closer toward our Why. Learning to accept and recognize that ahead of time has meant this period, which may have wiped me clean off the planet a few years ago, has been possible.

o o o

So we've established that we will not get it right all the time, and we're OK with that. But what can we do to maintain slowness in the face of those periods of busyness? How can we avoid overload, exhaustion, or even burnout?

Perhaps unsurprisingly, my answer is simply to pay attention.

For example, in the lead-up to Christmas this year, I'd moved too close to the edge of mindlessness. Not quite enough downtime, later nights, more skipping out on meditation, a higher workload as we prepared to close the office for a few weeks, more social events, more convenience foods, not enough intention. Years ago, I would have pushed through, ignoring the signs of overload, wondering why I ended up anxious and exhausted.

Now I recognize the way my breath sticks high in my chest, the way I'm inclined to stay up late, the way I will procrastinate at every option—and instead of spiraling into that overwhelming sense of *too much*, I check in with myself. Why am I feeling this way? What has changed? What is there more of? What is there less of?

I've become much better at recognizing the signs of a looming backslide and paying close attention to the areas of my life that have the greatest impact, ensuring they never slip too far out of hand.

Behavioral consultant Nicholas Bate refers to this regular checking in as "taking your MEDS," or, more specifically, paying attention to:

- mindfulness
- exercise
- diet
- sleep

Once I recognize which of these areas has changed, it's simpler (again, not necessarily easier) to recognize the issue and start fixing it. Sometimes the changes aren't in my control, so I need to look for ways of finding slow by creating more opportunities for a moment of deep breathing or paying close attention to what's in front of me. But other times, I've simply lost sight of what works, and it's a matter of adding more of those things I've neglected—mindfulness, simplicity, kindness—and reducing the things that don't serve me well.

Above all else, though, I simply go back to my Why.

I call to mind the foundation of this life I started unearthing in that

More of this, less of that

space	>	stuff
connection	>	comparison
learning	>	judging
mind-full	>	mind-less
love	>	likes
content	>	covet
friendship	>	followers
simple	>	complex
slow	>	fast
living	>	existing
you	>	the Joneses

apartment in the Canadian Rockies. The vivid imagining of a life well lived. The loved ones, the generosity, the adventure, and the world I want to leave behind. And if that feels too big (sometimes it feels too much like pressure), I call to mind even smaller reminders, like the warm pressure of my kids' hands in mine, the wholeness of a good conversation with Ben, the lightness of simply sitting quietly.

Our Why is the antidote to overload. It's a call back to the important things and a reminder that we don't need to carry the weight of everything—only those things that are important to us.

It's not about doing slow living perfectly. It's not about avoiding overload completely (as nice as that would be). Life is complicated, and we don't exist in a vacuum. A big practical part of slow living is building an awareness and learning how to combat the feeling of being overwhelmed before it takes over. Awareness and action. Noticing and evolving. Paying attention and making it count for something.

Questions to ask yourself if you start to feel overwhelmed: How are you feeling? Why are you feeling like that? What's changed? What is there more of? Stress? Commitments? Disconnection? Resentment? Hitting snooze? Eating crappy foods? Mindless consumption of social media, opinions, magazines, terrible TV, trends, fashion? What is there less of? Sleep? Meditation? Deep breathing? Drinking water? Saying no? Taking on the problems of others? Real connection?

nine

WHERE TO NOW?

■■ ■ ■ ■ ■ ■ ■ ■ ■ ▮ ■ ■ ■ ■ ■ ▮ ■ ■■

What if you've come to the end of this book and you want more? More inspiration, more action, more changes, more specifics? I get it. We want to be inspired, but we also want to know how to make specific changes. I think you and I have done a pretty good job of exploring the meaning behind slow living, as well as the importance of finding your own Why. But as we come to the final pages of this book, I want to tell you why it's important that the How of slow living comes from you.

S ince first emerging as the slow food movement in Italy in 1989—created in opposition to the rapid emergence of fast food (and fast living) and its resultant impact on health, local producers, and the environment—the idea of *slow* has expanded significantly. The foundation of slow remains the same—a return to high-quality basics, a reevaluation of the largely unnecessary "must-haves" of modern life, and a focus on going small, local, and community based. We now have slow parenting, slow art, slow travel, slow money, slow schools, and slow cities. And each of these movements represents a dizzying number of individual changes we could potentially make to our own ways of life.

So you'd be forgiven for picking up this book with the expectation of more. I certainly expected to cover more when I first sat down to write. Where's the sustainability advice, the green cleaning, the DIYs? Where are the recipes, the meditation instructions, the knitting? The natural fibers, the homemade bread, and the gentle color coordination? The rustic kitchen, the vintage caravan, the small-plot hobby farm?

The problem I realized quite quickly was that by putting all these together, to present them as *the* way to do slow living, is to paint a detailed portrait of a new set of Joneses.

This book is an introduction to the foundations of slow living—intention, simplicity, mindfulness, balance, connection—and enough examples of tiny, imperfect actions to encourage you to begin the journey, regardless of how small the step. I'd love you to use that foundation to create a slow life aligned with *your* values, rather than those of someone else.

Your version of slow living might include:

- sustainability
- waste-free living
- selling all your stuff and going on an adventure
- a tiny home
- permaculture
- quitting your job and starting something new
- slow travel

- changing your diet to reflect the slow food philosophy
- meditation
- yoga
- homeschooling
- self-sufficiency
- country living
- city living

These can all fit comfortably under the umbrella of slow, because slow living isn't a list of rules to abide by. Your version of slow living may well include an off-grid home in the countryside, hand-knitted socks, working remotely, camping trips, a big veggie garden, volunteering at the nearby nursing home, and a small brood of farm animals.

Or it could be a studio apartment in the middle of the city. Public transportation, farmers' markets, a sixty-hour week in a job you're passionate about, a vibrant group of interesting friends, an ethical wardrobe, ocean swimming twice a week, and meditation each night.

It might be a suburban home, two young kids, homemade bread in lunch boxes, music in the kitchen every day, cleaning with vinegar and baking soda, part-time work, a tight budget, secondhand clothes, Friday night pizza, and Sundays spent at the beach.

There is no version of slow living that can cover it all, and there isn't a person alive who could possibly cover all the bases all the time. Pretending that each of these elements of slow living shares a similar level of importance in my life would be peddling yet another unrealistic fantasy—if *only* you could achieve it, then everything would be great. Wonderful. Perfect, even!

But I hope I've convinced you that perfect doesn't exist, simple can actually be incredibly complex, and those Joneses down the street, well, they're not actually real. What does exist is honest, human, imperfect change. Every tiny step matters. Every time you make a seemingly insignificant shift toward your Why, every item you let go of, every deep breath, every kindness, every positive choice adds up to the creation of a life centered on what's important—to you.

○ ○ ○

I've found myself wondering how to conclude this book, how to place a bow on a gift we've only just opened. We can complicate the ideas of simple, slow living as much as we want. We can try to apply rules and guidelines and labels in order to understand it better. We can try to create a box in which it fits neatly, but there really is no tidy summation to this beautifully expansive idea of slow living other than this: be courageous in letting go.

When we let go of...

- stress
- tension
- clutter
- excess
- expectations
- shoulds
- obligations
- judgments
- ego

- ownership
- trying to please everyone
- specific outcomes
- total control
- perfectionism
- impossible standards
- being everywhere
- being everything to everyone

...we gain lightness, clarity, space, time, energy, purpose, compassion, acceptance. We allow ourselves to move forward. And slowly, we discover that contentment and simplicity lie on the other side.

When I began this journey toward a slower, simpler life, I clung to it as a life preserver. It was going to keep me afloat in a world of too much, help keep my head above water as all the commitments, expectations, and belongings tried to pull me under. It was a tool to use as I saw fit.

But it stirred things in me I never expected. It stirred an awakening and a noticing. It brought to the surface beauty and wonder and joy and emotions I couldn't even name. It was honesty and vulnerability and pain and creativity and love and identity.

It helped me to change not only the way I thought, the way I spent my time, the things I owned, the way I used technology, the food I cooked, the information I consumed, but also the way I viewed the world and the way I lived in it.

I learned that when we let go of the excess, the bullshit, the expectations, the trends, the clutter, the guilt—we strip away the blinkers. We remove the lens of ego from our eyes. We see more. We see others. We feel more deeply—the good and the bad. We care more fully. We love harder.

It's not just about letting go of clutter, learning to meditate, or creating a wardrobe we feel good wearing. It's about people and love and empathy and generosity and exploration. It's a call to humanity, our connection to each other, and all that we have to gain by opening our eyes. It's an invitation to *live*, not just exist.

And from that, I truly believe we can change the world. One small change, one act of letting go, one kindness, one connection, one tiny step forward every day.

Much of this book has been about me and my story. How I faltered and stumbled, how I discovered what works and what doesn't, how

I moved ahead and backslid. Some of it is direct, practical advice designed to help you unpack the ironic complexities of simplifying life, and throughout much of it, I encourage you to dig deep and gradually excavate your own Why. To examine the things that lie at the center of a life well lived and make an effort to move toward those things every day—one small, imperfect step at a time. But there's one other thing I want you to take from this book: permission.

You are allowed to make changes to the way you're living. You're allowed to look after yourself. You're allowed to decide what is important to you. And you're allowed to create a life with those things at the center.

It's OK to go slowly. It's OK to say no. It's OK to be different. And it's OK to let go of caring about the Joneses. Just don't replace them with a new set. Instead, create a life full of the things that matter to you, and watch as the world reveals beauty and humanity and connection. Slowly. Of course.

FURTHER INSPIRATION

Books

642 Tiny Things to Write About by The San Francisco Writer's Grotto

Yes Please by Amy Poehler

Bossypants by Tina Fey

Sick in the Head by Judd Apatow

To Kill a Mockingbird by Harper Lee

The Lorax by Dr. Seuss

Big Magic: Creative Living Beyond Fear by Elizabeth Gilbert

The Icarus Deception: How High Will You Fly? by Seth Godin

The Little Prince by Antoine de Sainte-Exupéry

Wool by Hugh Howey

The Stand by Stephen King

On Writing by Stephen King

The Dark Tower series by Stephen King

A Squash and a Squeeze by Julia Donaldson

Chasing Slow: Courage to Journey Off the Beaten Path by Erin Loechner

Tiny Beautiful Things: Advice on Love and Life from Dear Sugar by
    Cheryl Strayed

The Life-Changing Magic of Tidying Up by Marie Kondo

The Walking Dead series by Robert Kirkman, Charlie Adlard, and
    Cliff Rathburn

The MaddAddam trilogy by Margaret Atwood

Station Eleven by Emily St. John Mandel

The Hunger Games trilogy by Suzanne Collins

Websites

Zen Habits by Leo Babauta; zenhabits.net

The Art of Simple by Tsh Oxenreider; theartofsimple.net

Becoming Minimalist by Joshua Becker; becomingminimalist.com

Be More With Less by Courtney Carver; bemorewithless.com

Podcasts

Nerdist

WTF with Marc Maron

ACKNOWLEDGMENTS

T o everyone who has listened to *The Slow Home Podcast* (pogpast!), thank you. The fact that so many of us want to slow down, simplify, and spend more time on the things that matter is so exciting to me.

Thank you also to everyone at Allen & Unwin and the awesome team at Sourcebooks for your help, guidance, and support. A big thank you also to Adam Hollingworth for the cracking photos.

Thank you to all my friends—local, international, and digital—for understanding my need to disappear as I tilted in to writing this book.

Thank you to my big, wonderful family, who have given me my own roots and wings. My sisters, their husbands, their beautiful families, and my in-laws (and out-laws)—thank you for your unconditional love and laughs. An enormous thank you to Anne and Paul, the best parents-in-law you could ask for. And a completely inadequate thank you to my own parents, Pete and Bez. For your love, support, wisdom, and the reams of paper I used printing draft manuscripts while camped out at your house finishing this book—thank you.

Thank you most of all to my own wonderful family. Isla and Toby, thank you for reminding me to pay attention, to play every day, and to not take life too seriously. I love you both to the moon and back. Ben, thank you for it all: your endless support, early morning coffees, *Christmas Vacation* quotes, road trips, and willingness to take a grand plan and make it our adventure. Thank you most, though, for being next to me. I love you.

"For fast-acting relief, try slowing down."

—LILY TOMLIN

ABOUT THE AUTHOR

Brooke McAlary is a slow-traveling, gutsy, shiraz-appreciating writer who, after being diagnosed with severe postpartum depression in 2011, embarked on a one-woman mission to cut out the excess in her life and reconnect with what was really important. She is now immersed in the Slow Living philosophy and makes it her mission to help others define and achieve their slow living goals.

She writes the blog *Slow Your Home* and hosts and produces *The Slow Home Podcast*. She is currently slow-traveling her way around North America with her family.